MARTHA STEWART

WOMEN of ACHIEVEMENT

MARTHA STEWART

Charles J. Shields

CHELSEA HOUSE PUBLISHERS
PHILADELPHIA

Frontispiece: An accomplished gardener, cook, entertainer, decorator, and craftswoman, there seems little Martha Stewart cannot do or teach others to do. She is a self-avowed perfectionist whose life's work encompasses books, magazines, television shows, commercials, a website, newspaper column, radio show, mail-order catalogue, and several product lines.

Chelsea House Publishers
EDITOR IN CHIEF Sally Cheney
DIRECTOR OF PRODUCTION Kim Shinners
PRODUCTION MANAGER Pamela Loos
ART DIRECTOR Sara Davis
EDITOR Bill Conn
PRODUCTION EDITOR Diann Grasse
LAYOUT 21st Century Publishing and Communications, Inc.

The Chelsea House World Wide Web address is
http://www.chelseahouse.com

First Printing
1 3 5 7 9 8 6 4 2

CIP applied for
ISBN 0-7910-6318-4 (hc) — ISBN 0-7910-6319-4 (pbk)

CONTENTS

"Remember the Ladies"—Matina S. Horner   7

1.   The Wrong Spoons   13

2.   Growing Up in Nutley, New Jersey   19

3.   Trading Up   31

4.   Catering and Entertaining   43

5.   Single and "Living"   55

6.   Television to Time Magazine   67

7.   Just Desserts to Shares   79

8.   From Westport to Westchester County   87

9.   Looking Ahead   95

Chronology   103

Accomplishments   105

Further Reading   107

Index   108

WOMEN of ACHIEVEMENT

Jane Addams
SOCIAL WORKER

Madeleine Albright
STATESWOMAN

Marian Anderson
SINGER

Susan B. Anthony
WOMAN SUFFRAGIST

Joan of Arc
FRENCH SAINT AND HEROINE

Clara Barton
AMERICAN RED CROSS FOUNDER

Rachel Carson
BIOLOGIST AND AUTHOR

Cher
SINGER AND ACTRESS

Cleopatra
QUEEN OF EGYPT

Hillary Rodham Clinton
FIRST LADY AND ATTORNEY

Katie Couric
JOURNALIST

Diana, Princess of Wales
HUMANITARIAN

Emily Dickinson
POET

Elizabeth Dole
POLITICIAN

Amelia Earhart
AVIATOR

Gloria Estefan
SINGER

Jodie Foster
ACTRESS AND DIRECTOR

Ruth Bader Ginsburg
SUPREME COURT JUSTICE

Katherine Graham
PUBLISHER

Helen Hayes
ACTRESS

Mahalia Jackson
GOSPEL SINGER

Helen Keller
HUMANITARIAN

**Ann Landers/
Abigail Van Buren**
COLUMNISTS

Barbara McClintock
BIOLOGIST

Margaret Mead
ANTHROPOLOGIST

Julia Morgan
ARCHITECT

Toni Morrison
AUTHOR

Grandma Moses
PAINTER

Lucretia Mott
WOMAN SUFFRAGIST

Sandra Day O'Connor
SUPREME COURT JUSTICE

Rosie O'Donnell
ENTERTAINER AND COMEDIAN

Georgia O'Keeffe
PAINTER

Eleanor Roosevelt
DIPLOMAT AND HUMANITARIAN

Wilma Rudolph
CHAMPION ATHLETE

Diane Sawyer
JOURNALIST

Elizabeth Cady Stanton
WOMAN SUFFRAGIST

Martha Stewart
ENTREPRENEUR

Harriet Beecher Stowe
AUTHOR AND ABOLITIONIST

Barbra Streisand
ENTERTAINER

Amy Tan
AUTHOR

Elizabeth Taylor
ACTRESS AND ACTIVIST

Mother Teresa
HUMANITARIAN AND
RELIGIOUS LEADER

Barbara Walters
JOURNALIST

Edith Wharton
AUTHOR

Phillis Wheatley
POET

Oprah Winfrey
ENTERTAINER

"REMEMBER THE LADIES"

MATINA S. HORNER

"Remember the Ladies." That is what Abigail Adams wrote to her husband John, then a delegate to the Continental Congress, as the Founding Fathers met in Philadelphia to form a new nation in March of 1776. "Be more generous and favorable to them than your ancestors. Do not put such unlimited power in the hands of the Husbands. If particular care and attention is not paid to the Ladies," Abigail Adams warned, "we are determined to foment a Rebellion, and will not hold ourselves bound by any Laws in which we have no voice, or Representation."

The words of Abigail Adams, one of the earliest American advocates of women's rights, were prophetic. Because when we have not "remembered the ladies," they have, by their words and deeds, reminded us so forcefully of the omission that we cannot fail to remember them. For the history of American women is as interesting and varied as the history of our nation as a whole. American women have played an integral part in founding, settling, and building our country. Some we remember as remarkable women who—against great odds—achieved distinction in the public arena: Anne Hutchinson, who in the 17th century became a charismatic religious leader; Phillis Wheatley, an 18th-century black slave who became a poet; Susan B. Anthony, whose name is synonymous with the 19th-century women's rights movement, and who led the struggle to enfranchise women; and in the 20th century, Amelia Earhart, the first woman to cross the Atlantic Ocean by air.

These extraordinary women certainly merit our admiration, but other women, "common women," many of them all but forgotten, should also be recognized for their contributions to American thought and culture. Women have been community builders; they have founded schools and formed voluntary associations to help those in need; they have assumed the major responsibility for rearing children, passing on from one generation to the next the values that keep a culture alive. These and innumerable other contributions, once ignored, are now being recognized by scholars, students, and the public. It is exciting and gratifying that a part of our history that was hardly acknowledged a few generations ago is now being studied and brought to light.

In recent decades, the field of women's history has grown from obscurity to a politically controversial splinter movement to academic respectability, in many cases mainstreamed into such traditional disciplines as history, economics, and psychology. Scholars of women, both female and male, have organized research centers at such prestigious institutions as Wellesley College, Stanford University, and the University of California. Other notable centers for women's studies are the Center for the American Woman and Politics at the Eagleton Institute of Politics at Rutgers University; the Henry A. Murray Research Center for the Study of Lives, at Radcliffe College; and the Women's Research and Education Institute, the research arm of the Congressional Caucus on Women's Issues. Other scholars and public figures have established archives and libraries, such as the Schlesinger Library on the History of Women in America, at Radcliffe College, and the Sophia Smith Collection, at Smith College, to collect and preserve the written and tangible legacies of women.

From the initial donation of the Women's Rights Collection in 1943, the Schlesinger Library grew to encompass vast collections documenting the manifold accomplishments of American women. Simultaneously, the women's movement in general and the academic discipline of women's studies in particular also began with a narrow definition and gradually expanded their mandate. Early causes, such as woman suffrage and social reform, abolition, and organized labor were joined by newer concerns, such as the history of women in business and the professions and in politics and government; the study of the family; and social issues such as health policy and education.

Women, as historian Arthur M. Schlesinger, jr., once pointed out, "have constituted the most spectacular casualty of traditional history. They have made up at least half the human race, but you could never tell that by looking at the books historians write." The new breed of historians is remedying that omission. They have written books about immigrant women and about working-class women who struggled for survival in cities and about black women who met the challenges of life in rural areas. They are telling the stories of women who, despite the barriers of tradition and economics, became lawyers and doctors and public figures.

The women's studies movement has also led scholars to question traditional interpretations of their respective disciplines. For example, the study of war has traditionally been an exercise in military and political analysis, an examination of strategies planned and executed by men. But scholars of women's history have pointed out that wars have also been periods of tremendous change and even opportunity for women, because the very absence of men on the home front enabled them to expand their educational, economic, and professional activities and to assume leadership in their homes.

The early scholars of women's history showed a unique brand of courage in choosing to investigate new subjects and take new approaches to old ones. Often, like their subjects, they endured criticism and even ostracism by their academic colleagues. But their efforts have unquestionably been worthwhile, because with the publication of each new study and book another piece of the historical patchwork is sewn into place, revealing an increasingly comprehensive picture of the role of women in our rich and varied history.

Such books on groups of women are essential, but books that focus on the lives of individuals are equally indispensable. Biographies can be inspirational, offering their readers the example of people with vision who have looked outside themselves for their goals and have often struggled against great obstacles to achieve them. Marian Anderson, for instance, had to overcome racial bigotry in order to perfect her art and perform as a concert singer. Isadora Duncan defied the rules of classical dance to find true artistic freedom. Jane Addams had to break down society's notions of the proper role for women in order to create new social situations, notably the settlement house. All of these women had to come to terms both with themselves and with the world in which they lived. Only then could they move ahead as pioneers in their chosen callings.

Biography can inspire not only by adulation but also by realism. It helps us to see not only the qualities in others that we hope to emulate, but also, perhaps, the weaknesses that made them "human." By helping us identify with the subject on a more personal level they help us feel that we, too, can achieve such goals. We read about Eleanor Roosevelt, for instance, who occupied a unique and seemingly enviable position as the wife of the president. Yet we can sympathize with her inner dilemma; an inherently shy woman, she had to force herself to live a most public life in order to use her position to benefit others. We may not be able to imagine ourselves having the immense poetic talent of Emily Dickinson, but from her story we can understand the challenges faced by a creative woman who was expected to fulfill many family responsibilities. And though few of us will ever reach the level of athletic accomplishment displayed by Wilma Rudolph or Babe Zaharias, we can still appreciate their spirit, their overwhelming will to excel.

A biography is a multifaceted lens. It is first of all a magnification, the intimate examination of one particular life. But at the same time, it is a wide-angle lens, informing us about the world in which the subject lived. We come away from reading about one life knowing more about the social, political, and economic fabric of the time. It is for this reason, perhaps, that the great New England essayist Ralph Waldo Emerson wrote in 1841, "There is properly no history: only biography." And it is also why biography, and particularly women's biography, will continue to fascinate writers and readers alike.

"It's a good thing" has become Martha Stewart's catch phrase. She uses it to describe both her mass-market household merchandise and unique items only she uses, such as an expensive pair of Japanese gardening scissors. This simple motto also refers to the myriad skills and tasks Martha believes are worth doing well and the equipment needed to complete them.

THE WRONG SPOONS

I have set a standard, and I'm going to stick to the standard.

—Martha Stewart

Everything was all set. In February 1997 Martha Stewart and Floyd Hall, chief executive officer and president of Kmart, announced that Kmart's 2,100 outlets would soon be featuring Martha's World, a store within a store. Under the label Martha Stewart Everyday, Kmart would debut a new home collection of sheets, comforters, bed skirts, towels, and washcloths designed for bargain-minded shoppers looking for style and quality. They could find 230-thread-count sheets and plush 100 percent Egyptian cotton towels—at affordable prices. Also, Martha's World would offer 256 paint colors, specially selected by Stewart to complement her home furnishings. Stewart had her paint manufacturer concoct more than 2,000 colors, attempting to come up with color matches for everything from her cat's fur to the pastel eggs laid by her prized Araucana chickens.

"We know we have a winner," Hall said of the new line.

A great deal was riding on the venture. Immediately after the announcement, 3,000 vans loaded with Martha Stewart Everyday merchandise set out to stock the displays of 750 Kmart stores. Television commercials introducing the goods began airing right away. The TV ads were part of a $10 million national multimedia advertising campaign starring Martha Stewart.

Martha Stewart tried a partnership once before with Kmart, the country's second-largest discount store, but she said later, "I was not too happy. There was no quality control, which I needed for my grandiose plans for my department."

But Hall enticed her to return, explaining that he planned to spend $750 million streamlining and improving every store. Kmart market research determined that customers trusted Martha Stewart even more than their own doctors, and with that kind of support, Hall assured her that they could do a better job promoting Stewart's products this time around.

To kick off Martha's World in the media, Kmart sent special invitations to journalists from the Associated Press, *The New York Times*, *New York Post*, *Daily News*, *Newsday*, *Time* magazine, and various home and textile trade publications. The guests boarded a private jet and flew to Stewart's home in East Hampton, New York, the chic Long Island beach colony for summering Manhattanites.

At the town's Guild Hall, which Stewart had rented for the occasion, Stewart and Hall greeted everyone. Stewart explained that the goal of Martha's World was to put good taste and quality within reach of customers who probably didn't have much decorating experience—"those with a limited income, or who are frugal." As she explained it, "In every way, I am a teacher. We're going to bring along those customers who don't have the imagination to mix and match [fabric designs and patterns themselves]."

Next, the tour group moved on to Stewart's $1.5

million home on Lily Pond Lane. Why? "I have 13 bedrooms!" Stewart explained, enabling her guests to see the new line of bed and bath furnishings and some of the 256 "original" paint colors in the context of her own home.

Her classic shingled house on Lily Pond Lane is more than 100 years old and stands on a site formerly called Divinity Hill, named after the many ministers from New York and Brooklyn who boarded in her home and others on the lane. Stewart's house once belonged to a fiery preacher named the Rev. DeWitt Talmage, whose sermons in the city were attended by some 3,000 parishioners on any given Sunday. As Stewart squired the group around the grounds, she pointed out some of the renovations and improvements she'd made since buying the house five years before— one of which was a circular croquet court laid out within a square of rose bushes.

Then it was inside for a tour of the house. Stephen Drucker, the editor of *Martha Stewart Living* magazine, told the group that "Ms. Stewart loves East Hampton, and fashioned much of the 'look' of Martha Stewart Everyday from her sense of a classic East Hampton beach house." The group meandered through every bedroom and all five bathrooms, each one displaying examples of the Everyday line of sheets, comforters, shams, and bed skirts in ginghams and florals, madras designs and solids, with coordinating bath towels, bath rugs, shower curtains, and other accessories. Stewart's new line of Sherwin-Williams interior latex paint colors were also available to be viewed. Drucker chose color names—sandcastle, sunflower, Atlantic, and beach glass, among others—that denoted the local environment.

Finally, it was time for lunch.

In the dining room, everyone sat down to a meal of salmon, two salads, saffron risotto, and five different layer cakes—a feast that later appeared in the May edition

Martha Stewart, Chairman and CEO of Martha Stewart Living, worked with Chairman, President, and CEO of Kmart, Floyd Hall, to create "Martha's World" in 1997. This "store" within Kmart contains linens and home furnishing items in colors and patterns that recreate the atmosphere of an East Hampton beach house. Her line accounts for most of the household merchandise sold by the store.

of *Martha Stewart Living* magazine. But while everyone was eating and chatting, something happened.

In the midst of the perfectly planned, perfectly executed media event, Stewart—as the reporter for *Time* magazine noted—suddenly "displayed her temper, as famous as her zinnias, yelling at the help for setting out the wrong-size spoons."

"I'm a maniacal perfectionist," she once told Oprah Winfrey unapologetically in an interview for *O* magazine. "And if I weren't, I wouldn't have this company."

Perhaps not.

Martha Stewart has been called at different times the Queen of the Household, the Diva of Domesticity, and the High Priestess of Perfection. She has written 13 books, two of which have made the *New York Times* best-seller list. Her awarding-winning magazine, *Martha Stewart Living*, increased its circulation 10 times over, from 250,000 to 2.3 million in just seven years. Through her books and magazine, her Emmy-award winning television show, and her website, syndicated newspaper column, national radio show, mail-order catalog, and product lines, Martha Stewart has "had more influence on how Americans eat, entertain, and decorate their homes and gardens, than any one person in our history."

All this from someone raised in a lower-middle-class home in Nutley, New Jersey, who toyed with the idea of becoming a teacher when she was growing up, and wore dresses to high school that she sewed herself.

To anyone interested in finding out what kind of work ethic, abilities, and attitudes are needed to become a wealthy and influential businesswoman, the rise of Martha Stewart to building and owning an empire worth close to $1 billion offers fascinating lessons.

Martha as a teenager, the granddaughter of Polish immigrants. Friends and relatives report the crowded household was ruled by motivated, extremely strict, and sometimes quarrelsome parents. Her mother and father were college graduates, industrious, and skilled in domestic and household arts. They had great influence on Martha's future ambitions.

2

GROWING UP IN NUTLEY, NEW JERSEY

When I was young, I wanted to be a teacher.

—Martha Stewart

In August 1941—four months before the United States entered World War II following the bombing of Pearl Harbor—families in Jersey City, New Jersey, had steady money coming in and were grateful. After more than 10 years of the Great Depression, millions of men and women had lost their jobs due to cutbacks, and often when they had found other jobs they could not hold on to them for very long. Jersey City, located on the banks of the Hudson River, depended on its heavy industry, but for years a large share of its working-class men and women had been frequently left idle by the poor economy. The treadmill of hard times meant having to hustle for a regular paycheck.

So, Eddie Kostyra was lucky to have a secure job. Perhaps that's why he could afford to have his second child—Martha Helen Kostyra. She was born on Sunday, August 3, 1941, at Margaret Hague Maternity, a new hospital in Jersey City.

Eddie Kostyra, the 28-year-old son of Polish immigrants, was a physical-education teacher. He had spent his childhood living above the tavern that his parents owned. Eddie was bright and creative, and had a flair for music, which he demonstrated as the drum major for his high-school marching band. At one time he had thought about becoming a doctor, but had to settle for being a teacher. In those days, he was fortunate to go to college at all and, furthermore, to be able to become a professional when many men earned their pay as laborers.

He was good-looking—six feet tall, athletic, blond with blue eyes—and when he met 22-year-old Martha Ruszkowski at a Polish-heritage seminar in 1937, she caught his eye. The two were married not long after. His young bride also had a teaching certificate, although the arrival of two babies in the first four years of marriage kept her at home. Like most Catholic women of her generation, she accepted babies and motherhood as they came. In fact, she would have her sixth and last baby when she was 41.

A few days after baby Martha was born, she came home to live with her parents and older brother, Eric, still a toddler, in a cramped ground-floor flat shared with three other families. As young parents, the Kostyras could count on a few things in their favor that would help them weather the end of the Depression—and the upcoming World War—better than many people. In addition to having teaching backgrounds, the two were also knowledgeable about "domestic arts," or home economics, as it was later called. Eddie was unique in that his mother had taught him how to cook, sew, and garden, in the hope of encouraging his creative side.

Martha Kostyra, too, had been taught those skills as a child, though out of necessity. She was a skilled seamstress, adept at making dresses and selling them to relatives and neighbors. Her father had been an ironworker—a backbreaking, low-paying trade—in

Buffalo, New York, all of his life. Years later Mrs. Kostyra confided to one of her children that she had grown up "with nothing," and marrying Eddie was her first chance at living a middle-class life.

In 1944, when Martha was three, the Kostyra family moved to their own home at 86 Elm Place in Nutley, New Jersey—a two-story, three-bedroom, one-bathroom house with a full basement, sun room, sewing room, unfinished attic, and room for a garden in the backyard. Years later Martha Stewart would devote many of her "Remembering" columns in *Martha Stewart Living* magazine to her experiences growing up at 86 Elm Place. Like some of the television programs about families she enjoyed watching as a child in the 1950s, she paints a portrait of the Kostyras living together in a warm and comfortable household.

The modest three-bedroom family home of the Kostyra's at 86 Elm Place, Nutley, New Jersey is a far cry from the numerous, large estates Martha would eventually own. She reminisces about her days in Nutley in her current magazine column, perhaps remembering that time more favorably than actually experienced.

However, friends and neighbors, and even her siblings, recall a different atmosphere.

As a father, Eddie Kostyra was "very difficult, very demanding," which even Stewart admits. Self-betterment mattered to him, and he expected that attitude in his children, too. While teaching, he took night classes. Then, not long after moving his family to Nutley, he became a pharmaceutical salesman. The family trooped off to Mass every Sunday, and as his sons got older, Eddie put them in Cub Scouts, even becoming a prominent Scout leader himself. He pored over issues of *National Geographic,* priding himself on knowing something about all sorts of topics. He even set up a little lab in the basement where he experimented with fertilizer formulas for growing bigger tomatoes. Before Martha even entered school, he showed her how to take care of a garden. "I was *trained* to be productive," Martha told Oprah Winfrey in an interview.

Eddie fought loudly and angrily with his wife, too. Though Mr. and Mrs. Kostyra often argued in Polish when they didn't want the children to understand, the pushing and sometimes slapping couldn't be misinterpreted. Despite the tension in the house—made worse by the family expanding to six children and two adults in three bedrooms—Martha recalls the rule of the house: Don't cry. (The message stuck. As head of a business employing nearly 500 people, Stewart once told one of her creative directors when she found the woman in tears, "Guess what? No crying.")

To escape the pressures of her father—a "crazy force in the family," she once called him—Martha turned to the haven of learning.

She attended Yantacaw Elementary School, where she excelled at spelling tests and practically any academic subject where sheer persistence earned high marks. Then in the third grade, Martha latched on to a role model: her teacher, Irene Weyer. Miss Weyer lavished her with the praise and attention she craved.

"She was special because she took time and cared for each of her students," Martha said. "There wasn't a moment that wasn't devoted to her children, as she called them. She was a spinster, but that never deterred her in her love of all the other children. In fact, I think it made her more [capable of loving]. And she was fair, but she was stern. She was strict, but she was forgiving. She was the ideal teacher to me." And in direct contrast to the atmosphere in Martha's home, Miss Weyer's classroom was "full of laughter and fun." A photograph of Miss Weyer's class shows Martha sitting front and center.

But another side to her teacher also appealed to nine-year-old Martha. Miss Weyer prided herself on looking

Two teachers at Yantacaw Elementary School provided the ideal of the perfect woman for Martha: calm, well-dressed, and successful. Martha's voracious reading, good grades, and academic awards at this school showed the beginnings of her disciplined nature. And her first jobs of babysitting and selling baked goods showed the beginnings of her business interests.

well dressed, feminine, and professional every day—
"beautifully groomed," as Stewart recalled in one of
her magazine columns. To her admiring pupil, whose
own dresses were pretty but handmade, Miss Weyer
presented a picture of success and self-assurance in her
stylish outfits. A bond formed between the two that
lasted for years. In middle and high school, Martha
stopped by to see Miss Weyer now and then, bringing
her up to date on how one of her favorite students
was doing.

In the fifth grade Martha found a second role model,
Miss Mitchell, who had in common with Miss Weyer
many of the qualities Martha respected. Stewart
remembers Miss Mitchell as a "family person, someone
who shared her students with other teachers because we
started to have moving classes in fifth grade. In fifth
and sixth grade you traveled from one room to another
to study the different subjects. And she would share,
and she was fair. It's the fairness and the ability to listen
and to answer questions that I really find very, very
important with teaching."

The second refuge for a girl drawn to learning and
the possibilities of life was the Nutley Public Library.
Built around the time of the First World War in the
early part of the 20th century, the Nutley Public
Library was already an important institution of the
town when Martha discovered it. It also had a special
children's section. Fortunately Eddie Kostyra, a regular
reader himself, believed that time spent in a book was
worthwhile. "We had a lot of chores at our house, a
tremendous number of chores," Stewart said, "but we
were always granted the time to read."

In the third grade Martha won a library contest for a
perfect score on a test given after students read a pre-
scribed number of books and answered questions about
them correctly. Now not only could she wander around
the children's section, but winning the contest meant
being given special access to the adult section—the

Stockton Room—too. "In the adult library I had to be more choosy because there were so many books. But I would talk to the librarians, I would get suggestions, I would read the book reviews, I would find out what I should be reading."

Martha found herself drawn to classic novels and biographies of people who chased success and caught it. She had a favorite reading chair, though sometimes she read sitting in a tree where she could be left alone. "On Sunday mornings, because we had such chaos around our house, everybody running and getting dressed to go to church and everything, I sat in the car and read. I read everything. I read from A to Z in the Stockton Room. I just started on the As and went all the way through," she said.

Not all the subject matter she chose was weighty and uplifting, either. Friends in middle school recall her also reading popular romances aimed at girls, books about student nurses and dating and mysteries, such as the famous *Nancy Drew* books. In high school she joined thousands of other teenagers who read the novel *Peyton Place*, published in 1956 when she was 14. Written by Grace Metalious with bare-knuckled candor about sex in a small New England town, *Peyton Place* was considered so shocking and inappropriate that Canada banned its import, and a library in Beverly Farms, Massachusetts, even posted a sign outside: "This library does not carry *Peyton Place*. If you want it, go to Salem." Martha covered her copy in brown paper so that no one would know what she was reading.

But although her love of reading often allowed Martha to escape her situation at home, the birth of her sister Laura when Martha was a teenager squeezed the household even tighter. Martha already shared a room with sister Kathy, and a small bureau was the only space available for her pins, barrettes, combs, and other accessories. Friends remember her complaining about having to wash her hair in the bathroom sink, where signs of teeth-brushing were everywhere. Unable to afford new clothes most of the time, she made her own.

She disliked home economics in middle school, though, mainly because, as she told friends, she already had to cook, clean, and sew at home. To get spending money for things she wanted, she baby-sat and even started a little neighborhood catering business, picking up tips from an elderly couple—retired bakers—who lived next door. It was her first attempt at a business that would later make her a millionaire many times over.

She also began modeling. Teenage fashion was turning into a big business for the first time in the 1950s, and, like many girls, Martha had heard that modeling paid well. It was a sign of unusual self-confidence that a girl from an ethnic background with a strong New Jersey accent—and a "beanpole" figure according to one of her dates—with no wardrobe of the latest fashions to wear, would take a stab at modeling, but she set off determinedly.

Her father, always one to encourage such ambition, provided her with a basic portfolio. Although not a professional photographer, he did his best to capture her angular but expressive face. Then, accompanied by a friend, Martha boarded the bus headed for the Port Authority Terminal in midtown Manhattan, then traveled downtown, where she made the rounds of modeling agents—though apparently never going after the top agencies.

Eventually, at just 13 years old, she landed a job, modeling on Saturdays for Bonwit Teller, an upscale women's store in the heart of Manhattan. In her junior year at Nutley High School, she astounded classmates by appearing in a national soap commercial that aired during prime time on Saturday night. Although her friends were amused by how her "New Joisey"-accented voice had been overdubbed with someone

else's, nevertheless, Marty—as some of her friends had nicknamed her—already a grade getter, was clearly turning into a go-getter as well.

The importance of work and success was a topic Martha and her father could agree on, and it seems to have led to good times between them. Her dad even helped decorate her high-school gym for the prom during her junior year. And despite homework and chores, Martha could often be found sitting in the kitchen with her father, talking for hours, some nights quite late, munching white-bread sandwiches of mustard, onions, and butter. In her magazine columns, Stewart recalls a springtime ritual of examining seed catalogs with her father and planning the garden.

Nutley High School, New Jersey, where Martha wore her homemade dresses. She became an expert at "making do" with what her family could afford, and was trained from a very early age to be a provider. During her teen years, Martha's social life and dating were secondary to her grades, chores, and work.

On one subject, however, her father could not be moved, and that was boys. Word spread around Nutley High School that dating Martha Kostyra meant dealing with Mr. Kostyra. Some boys joked that if you got Martha home late, you'd better slow down just long enough to let her out because Mr. Kostyra would be in the front yard, waiting. But boyfriends didn't figure very importantly in the picture, anyway. Except for the occasional dances—she was crowned Sweetheart of Xavier High, where her date was enrolled as a military cadet— Martha led a life devoted primarily to schoolwork, responsibilities at home, and earning money for college. Graduating in the upper 10 percent of her class—she had attended her senior prom in a dress she'd made from a pattern in *Vogue*—Martha was thrilled when she received a Rotary Club scholarship, which paid part of her tuition at her first-choice school, Barnard College, an all-women's college in New York City and one of the original "Seven Sisters" of the Ivy League colleges. Martha's hard work was already beginning to pay off.

Her books and magazines have been praised for showing a cheerful, pleasant portrait of domesticity. Martha herself graduated college in 1964, became a mother a year later, and then went to work on Wall Street in the early 1970s. But her own experience of being a working mom was not so tranquil, ". . . Women went to work, they went crazy . . . They thought the family could wait. And you know what? The family can't wait."

3

TRADING UP

When I got married and had a child and went to work, my day was all day, all night. You lose your sense of balance.

—Martha Stewart

Barnard College in 1959 was an adventurous choice for a young woman raised in a conservative Polish Catholic family. Founded in 1889 as one of the few colleges in the nation where women could receive the same rigorous education available to men, Barnard is located in uptown Manhattan, a stone's throw from Central Park, directly across Broadway from Columbia University, with which it is affiliated. Even today, Barnard's website proclaims, "[W]ith a more than 110-year tradition as an independent women's college . . . Barnard continues to challenge the way its students think about themselves, their world, and their roles in changing it."

"I applied to some nice colleges [including] Stanford," Martha told Oprah Winfrey in *O* magazine, "and then I realized, I can't go to Stanford; it's across the country! I didn't have enough money to go away, though I'd love to know what my life would be like if I'd gone to Stanford. It would have been a very different life. I wanted to stay in New York—that's why I went to Barnard College, which was, to me, the best college I could go to."

In the '60s, as well as today, Barnard was strong in both the humanities and the sciences, areas of study that interested Martha. In fact, she planned to study chemistry—her father fancied himself an amateur chemist—but she eventually switched to a combined major of art, European, and architectural history.

In addition to Barnard's academic strengths, New York was in its heyday as the cultural capital of the United States, and no doubt Martha, like many young people at the time, thrilled to the idea of rubbing elbows with the trendsetters in fashion, art, music, and literature. "New York is our laboratory," boasted Columbia's college catalogue. Greenwich Village, in particular—just a subway ride downtown from Barnard and Columbia—held legendary appeal as an artsy neighborhood of coffeehouses, poetry readings, and jazz performances. Martha explored the winding streets of the Village on a few dates. Dan Wakefield, a popular writer of the day, recalled:

> There was a quietness about [Greenwich Village], almost a hush, compared to the taxi-blasting traffic, street crowds, and vendors of Broadway, midtown, and Morningside Heights. The special quiet of the Village suggested creation rather than commerce and conveyed a tone of mystery. That aura was added to by the places hidden away like the prizes on a treasure hunt. . . . You opened the door to a warm room lit by a fireplace, where Village denizens drank and ate at wooden tables surrounded by a frieze of faded dust jackets on the walls, from books by the writers who frequented the place in the twenties and thirties. It was like walking into a wonderful secret and becoming part of it, taking your place in the play.

Unfortunately, Martha's "place in the play" was limited by her lack of money. Despite her scholarship, she couldn't afford to live on campus her freshman year. Instead, every day she boarded a bus in Nutley, got off at the Port Authority Terminal, and then rode the subway to 116th street at the edge of campus.

Barnard required undergraduates to take a heavy load of five courses the first semester. Just earning passing grades freshman year was most girls' goal. But because of her financial straits, Martha also had to continue modeling part-time. Using the two-hour commute to do some of her homework, she rushed off between classes to modeling jobs. "Tall, angular and pleasingly all-American, she wasn't supermodel material, but she was stylish and looked good in front of a camera," commented writer Kate Moses in the e-zine, *Salon.com*. Friends filled out her wardrobe by lending her clothes.

One day in the spring of 1960, while Martha was browsing for books in the Barnard library, another student approached her. Diane Stewart had seen Martha in an art class and was impressed by her looks and poise. Diane showed Martha a picture of her brother and offered to arrange a date. They traded phone numbers and Martha waited, as was the iron-clad tradition in those days, "for the boy to call."

The "boy," Andy Stewart, was three and a half years older than Martha. He was a graduate of University of Virginia with a degree in philosophy, and had just started Yale Law School in New Haven, Connecticut. Andy was the product of a rather eccentric home. His father, an independently wealthy stockbroker in New York, spent money lavishly. Andy's parents loved to travel, and when the spirit seized them, they pulled up stakes and took off. Andy had received a fragmented education in Europe and New England, experiencing school environments that varied from being straight-laced to extremely lenient. The secondary school he'd graduated from, the Putney School in Vermont, was run like a combination camp, commune, and college. Added to these circumstances, his mother was—as Martha later put it—"quite an infamous interior designer." The family lived at different times in more than half a dozen apartments in Manhattan, each one decorated in Mrs. Stewart's sense of high style, which favored mirrors, heavy drapes, and rich upholstery like an 18th-century French chateau.

That spring of 1960, Martha worked as a live-in maid for a pair of sisters on Fifth Avenue and lived in the servants' quarters. When Andy and Martha met, it was probably a case of opposites attracting.

When Andy picked her up at the swank address, he had a toothache. Martha eased the tension between the two by teasing Andy about it. He liked her confidence and directness. Later that spring he told her he had planned to spend the summer traveling abroad and asked her to join him somehow. But it was out of the question on the meager wages she was making, even with help from occasional modeling jobs.

After months of separation during the summer, they spent much of their spare time together again that fall, with Andy sometimes paying Martha's train fare to New Haven. At Christmas Martha brought Andy home to Nutley to meet her parents. But Eddie Kostyra had suspicions about young men—especially young men who weren't Catholic—and the visit didn't go smoothly. Regardless, Andy proposed to Martha in February 1961.

Meanwhile, Martha had scored a major victory when *Glamour* magazine chose her as one of the "ten best-dressed college girls in America" on the basis of photographs she submitted to the contest sporting dressy, casual, and business outfits—all of them borrowed. In the pages of *Glamour*, the 5' 9" college student appeared in a full-page black-and-white layout, posing a little stiffly in an A-line coat, heels, gloves, and alligator handbag—all no doubt supplied by the fashion editor—with the text praising her "tenderness" and "vitality."

Winning the *Glamour* contest gave her modeling career a real boost—it even led to a profile in the French magazine *Marie Claire*—so when Andy proposed, Martha hesitated. After all, there was even a

Martha, in elegant evening wear. A much different situation from 1961, when she was photographed in clothes borrowed from college friends for a "Best-Dressed College Girls" contest with Glamour *magazine. Always looking for a way around obstacles, she didn't let the lack of her own clothing deter her. Winning the contest helped Martha's modeling career.*

possibility that she might be invited to Paris for a photo shoot, which might lead to other high-paying assignments. Within a month, however, she accepted Andy's proposal, and the couple were formally engaged in March. The pair set a date for July 1, 1961, following the end of Martha's sophomore year.

The wedding was simple; apparently her family did not pick up much of the tab—not surprising in light of the fact that Eddie Kostyra made it known that he was not happy about the impact the marriage would have on his daughter's life. Martha sent out handwritten invitations to a simple ceremony in St. Paul's Chapel at Columbia University; she made her own wedding dress with help from her mother; and as she walked down the aisle one month shy of her 20th birthday, she carried a bouquet of freshly picked daises. There was no official wedding photographer.

After a weekend getaway honeymoon in Vermont, the newlyweds spent one day moving their belongings into an apartment lent to them for the summer by one of Andy's friends. Andy had a summer job clerking in a law firm, and Martha kept hitting the modeling circuit. But when fall came around again, Andy had to return to New Haven to complete his final year in law school, and rather than be apart from him, Martha agreed to take a year off from school. They moved into a small house in Milford, Connecticut—not far from the Yale campus—which they shared with another couple.

For Thanksgiving, Martha attempted her first holiday meal as a young bride. It was a disaster—[the opposite of what we would expect from the Martha Stewart of today]. She burned the turkey. Relatives arrived expecting to eat dinner in the early afternoon, but it wasn't ready until after dark.

In June 1962 Andy graduated from Yale with a law degree and enrolled in graduate studies at Columbia University. Sticking to their plan, Martha reenrolled at Barnard to finish her final year. Like most married students budgeting on a shoestring, they were forced to take an apartment whose only selling point was that it was better than nothing. Martha tried to fix up the place with furniture donated by friends. She even purchased a few parakeets in an attempt to make the rooms cheerier. But years later she admitted in a *USA Today* interview that the apartment was "three miserable rooms overlooking the rooftops of 114th Street."

Andy finally finished graduate work in law at Columbia

University in January 1964. With just a thesis standing between her and a degree, Martha would be graduating from Barnard the following June, so the couple celebrated by touring Europe. Money from the advertisements Martha had appeared in for big brand names such as Breck and Clairol hair products, Lifebouy soap, and Tareyton cigarettes (although Martha was a nonsmoker) came in handy. They traveled around Italy, France, and Germany, dining in cafés and restaurants and plying the waiters and chefs with questions about the food, which Martha later called the beginning of her "serious culinary education."

She started her "serious culinary education" while on a European vacation with husband, Andy, in 1964. There, Martha dined in several excellent restaurants and asked numerous questions of the waiters and chefs, such as those pictured here, about the food. As usual, she seized every available opportunity to learn.

Upon their return, Martha graduated in June 1964 with a degree in art history, and the Stewarts—banking on the income Andy could expect as an attorney—splurged by renting an upscale six-room apartment on Riverside Drive with a view of the Hudson River. This time the couple decorated the place with all the time and energy that they could devote to it. Martha's mother-in-law tipped her off to the best antique auctions and taught her how to bid. Before long, Martha said, "I learned all the sources, the bargain hunting, the auctions, and I developed an affinity for interior design, color, all the stuff I deal in now."

The Stewarts had friends over for dinner regularly, and Martha began experimenting with various menus, including theme dinners. A typical cookbook of the day, introducing a "Hawaiian dinner party at home" gushes, "You're never quite the same again, once you've tasted the cosmopolitan cuisine that flourishes amid the palms." The menu calls for avocado cocktail, lobster curry, baked bananas, green salad tossed with herbs, papaya with sherbet, and Kona coffee—not so unusual now but exotic fare during the 1960s.

A little more than a year after the Stewarts settled down, their daughter, Alexis, was born on September 27, 1965. Her parents nicknamed her Lexi, and Martha waited until the baby was three months old before modeling again. A young actress living in the building (Valerie Harper, who later became a regular on the *Mary Tyler Moore Show*) baby-sat while Martha went out for appointments and assignments. But eventually the young mother decided to drop modeling altogether. Instead, having fallen in love with a 19th-century schoolhouse they found near Middlefield in western Massachusetts, the Stewarts decided to make rehabbing the property a family project.

The task was formidable. The schoolhouse had no modern improvements and badly needed landscaping. Moreover, the round-trip from New York to Middlefield was six hours in good weather. Regardless, the Stewarts brought to bear on the Middlefield house all the traits that would later become emblems of their work ethic, particularly Martha's. With relentless energy, Martha insisted things were done right and in the way they wanted. Weekend after weekend the Stewarts made the long trip, spent all day Saturday and Sunday sanding, painting, hammering, and digging, then drove back late, sometimes with vegetables from their garden for friends. It would take five years to completely restore and improve the property.

As if this weren't enough, Martha then decided she was ready for yet another challenge. "The first thing that really caught me [after college]," she said, "was the stock market."

A family friend suggested that her personality was suited to selling stocks on Wall Street. However, she first had to pass an exam required of all stockbrokers, so she buckled down for three months of study and passed. A small firm hired her, impressed by her go-getter attitude, and soon she was doing quite well. While Lexi stayed in the care of a woman hired to look after her, Martha began pulling down deals that earned her 10 times the annual income that most middle-class Americans were receiving in the early 1970s. But more importantly, she was learning the ropes of big business and its key elements—investment, negotiation, and corporate finance. Writer Mary Elizabeth Williams, in her *Salon* essay, "She's Martha and You're Not," remarked that Wall Street was a perfect fit for Martha: "It was yet another gear in the machine that would become Martha Inc., and a chance for her to temper her homey skills and pretty-face image with some serious business savvy. On Wall Street, Martha cultivated her competitive, aggressive salesmanship and got her first real taste of power."

In 1973, however, the stock market plunged deeply into negative numbers. Several of Martha's friends for whom she'd served as investment adviser lost money. On a trip to Boston she was shocked by a newspaper article reporting that a company she was planning on endorsing that very day had been hit hard. Apparently the days of fun and excitement on Wall Street were ending—at least temporarily. Added to this, Martha may have been having second thoughts about the time spent away from her husband and daughter. Later she said, "When I got married and had a child and went to work, my day was all day, all night. You lose your sense of balance. That was in the late '60s, '70s, women went to work, they went crazy. They thought the workplace was much more exciting than the home. They thought the family could wait. And you know what? The family can't wait."

She resigned from the firm, saying later in an interview that she knew she would miss the atmosphere of being around bright, assertive people. "It was hard to leave Wall Street," she said. "My associates were extremely interesting. They were readers, book buyers, art collectors—raconteurs." One of her co-workers was Brian Dennehy, who at 40 became a movie actor and later an award-winning stage actor.

In any case, the Stewarts were already in another "fixer-upper" project, having sold the renovated schoolhouse in Middlefield. This time they purchased an abandoned 1805 farmhouse in Westport, Connecticut, perched on Turkey Hill.

Town residents called the weathered, deteriorating hulk the "Westport Horror." But in less than a decade, under Martha's determined guidance her home would become the heart of her catering business, later recognized by millions as the beautiful backdrop for best-selling cooking, decorating, and gardening books—an environment of graciousness and good taste. In her own words, Turkey Hill would become "an icon of American living."

A Christmas wreath for a window of Martha's home, Turkey Hill, in Westport, CT. The original renovation of Turkey Hill took 10 years. She began her first commercial enterprise here, a successful catering business. The estate was both Martha's laboratory and proving ground, and later became a studio backdrop for television programs and printed photo spreads.

4

CATERING AND ENTERTAINING

The big, big turning point was when I wrote my first book. Americans look at you very differently, respect you greatly more when you write a book.

—Martha Stewart

Westport, Connecticut, is a shorefront town that stretches north into wooded hills and south to Long Island Sound. It was once an artists' colony, attracting creative people who gravitated to a sophisticated small town that suited their personalities. Even today, Westport is home to many professionals in the arts—theater, publishing, fine arts, and television. Its location is convenient, too, with New York City only an hour away by car or train.

Still, the Stewarts' friends must have been a little surprised when Andy and Martha announced in the spring of 1971 that they were moving out of their six-room Manhattan apartment and relocating to a small town in Connecticut. Even if Wesport did have a reputation as a lovely place to live, Martha was still working as a Wall Street stockbroker—at least for another year, and Andy's law practice was in Manhattan, too. Moreover, they had put a lot of "sweat equity" into the schoolhouse in Middlefield, and now they had sold that showplace to tackle a big, drafty hulk of a house that needed a complete overhaul. And despite the amount of work involved, they had already decided that they weren't going to call in a small army of hammer-and-saw tradespeople to help them, either. They would do most of it themselves.

Turkey Hill—the house, outbuildings, and grounds —was in bad shape. Yet the Stewarts further increased their workload by purchasing neighboring lots and adding to the size of their property. Before they even officially moved in, they planted an orchard with 45 fruit trees (which are difficult to care for), among them apple, sour cherry, quince, pear, plum, and white peach. Half an acre became a garden for vegetables, herbs, and blueberries. A second large parcel of land was turned into a flower garden. They installed a distinctive black-bottom swimming pool, added a second barn, a hen house, and beehives. Chickens, turkeys, geese, baby goats, tens of thousands of bees, and one black sheep took up residence.

Years later the animals, orchard, and gardens were used as proof in a legal wrangle involving Martha. A gardener sued her for overtime pay, but Martha successfully argued through her attorney that her property was actually a working farm. By that definition her former employee was an agricultural worker and therefore not entitled to overtime pay.

Slowly Turkey Hill's landscape began to assume the look of a small country estate right out of New England's past. As if expressing her feelings of permanence about the place, Martha built a long stone wall that she was especially proud of—though, interestingly, much later she interpreted the number of stone walls cropping up in her neighborhood as a sign of unfriendliness.

The grounds of the reno-vated house at Westport held room enough for a fruit orchard, vegetable garden, flower garden, swimming pool, two barns, hen house, beehives, and a menagerie of pets. Martha is shown with a beloved Chow dog, just one of 13 dogs and cats that she groomed regularly every week.

Progress on the interior of the house, of course, was another story. Amid plastic sheets hanging down where walls had once been, wood floorboards whitened by plaster dust, and piles of interior remodeling tools stacked in corners, the Stewarts got ready every Monday through Friday morning for their jobs as high-powered professionals in New York City. Then on evenings and weekends, they went back to scraping, sanding, spackling, drilling, staining, and painting. For two years they didn't invite anyone over for dinner or parties. After Martha left the investment firm and

Alexis was in school, she devoted herself to working on the house full-time.

With the improvements to the house came a sub-family of household pets. At one time, the Stewarts owned nine cats and four butterscotch-colored chow dogs known for their thick, fluffy fur and dark-blue tongues. Martha groomed all of them every Saturday.

Once the kitchen was finished, Martha eagerly fired it up. She held cooking classes for friends' and neighbors' children, gathering the seven- and eight-year-olds around the table and stove to demonstrate how to make simple desserts and treats.

Then she spied her first opportunity for connecting cooking with business.

The Common Market in Westport was a string of fashionable shops with a small food court where shoppers could rest and have a cup of coffee and something to nibble on. But Martha imagined turning the food court into a cozy atmosphere where baked goods could be showcased. She approached the owners and offered to manage the shop and supply it with her own array of cookies, breads, and pastries. In her pitch she played a clever card: she invited them to her dazzling Turkey Hill kitchen to demonstrate what she could do. (Apparently a misunderstanding arose about who was going to do the actual baking, though, because Martha later hired local women to bake in their own kitchens, which the owners later claimed they never agreed to.) She got the job, and the Market Basket, as Martha renamed the business, was a hit. For three years its reputation grew while Martha fine-tuned her perceptions of how to delight people. She also introduced antiques and other furnishings that gave the shop its particular charm.

Meanwhile, Andy's career had taken a new direction as well. In early 1976 he left behind representing a caseload of clients and became instead a general legal counsel to Henry R. Abrams, a respected publisher. Abrams had earned a lucrative spot in publishing as a creator of what are called coffee-table books, usually large, expensively produced, and lavishly illustrated books on general topics like antique cars or ancient temples of the world. As a career move, publishing was evidently a perfect fit for Andy. Before long he was promoted to president and then chief executive officer. Under Andy's guidance, the company scored a best-seller hit with *Gnomes*, a book about imaginary little people, written in the Netherlands but translated and packaged for sale in the United States.

With Martha's entrepreneurial spirit fueling the Market Basket and Andy's energies being poured into Henry R. Abrams, it's probably safe to assume that the couple was constantly on the go. Added to their professional lives, of course, was Turkey Hill, the small estate being literally brought back to life under their own hands.

The Stewarts' combined stress ratcheted up a notch when Martha decided to use her customer contacts at the Market Basket to promote her own catering business.

Realizing that many of the same qualities that had made the Market Basket a success could be transferred to garden parties, weddings, receptions, anniversary dinners—all sorts of occasions when food should be elegantly presented—Martha advertised her services as a caterer. Her first job was a wedding with 300 guests. On a sweltering day with the temperature hovering around 100 degrees Fahrenheit, Martha stood smiling underneath a banquet tent beside a table of delicacies, hoping no one would notice that some of the desserts were melting and sliding sideways.

Still, the wedding was a success, and the demand for her services soon exploded. Martha severed her relationship with the Market Basket. (She had briefly tried opening a retail store in Westport featuring specialty foods and supplies for entertaining, but she lacked serious investors.) She went into partnership with Norma Collier, a friend from college, and the

by Craig Claibourne; *The Fannie Farmer Cookbook*; Irma S. Rombauer and Marion Rombauer Becker's *Joy of Cooking*; Peg Bracken's funny anti-cookbook, *I Hate to Cook Book*; and any number of the books written for the *House & Garden* series by the "Father of American Cooking," James Beard. For adventurous souls there were collections of recipes from famous restaurants or books by the flamboyant and much-loved chef Julia Child. But in general the cookbook-buying audience was thought to be limited—mainly because American cuisine at the time was also limited. Even cooking shows on television, with the exception of Julia Childs's, seemed to be promoting the idea that cooking was a hobby and a practical skill but nothing more.

Martha Stewart changed all that, expanding the preparation of food, its presentation, and even the atmosphere surrounding it into a visual experience, the way a wedding has a special look to it. Perhaps her modeling background influenced her emphasis on appearance as a big part of appeal.

Immediately, for instance, she broke the mold by refusing to go along on a key point with her publisher, Clarkson N. Potter, Crown's lifestyle division. The Clarkson Potter editors, adhering to the layout and design of most cookbooks up to that time, wanted black-and-white printing and graphics throughout. After all, a cookbook was pretty much one page after another of recipes, wasn't it? But Martha insisted on color—lots of it. Moreover, she wanted a sumptuous design that would make just paging through the book an experience in itself. If this required expensive paper—which it would—so be it.

First, however, the book's text had to be written. Surprisingly, Martha Stewart does not pretend to have a major interest in writing. Despite working with various magazines during her career, she has said on several occasions that writing is hard and boring for her. So in creating the text of her first book, *Entertaining*, she turned to a professional—Elizabeth Hawes.

Hawes was a freelance writer who had been published in the *New Yorker* magazine, one of the most highly regarded magazines for prose fiction, poetry, and nonfiction. She and Stewart were friends, and in enlisting her help, Martha made the arrangement on a friendly basis. They would write the book together, and Hawes would get a flat fee.

Meeting usually at Turkey Hill, Elizabeth prodded Stewart for stories about her cooking experiences, from growing up in Nutley to serving up a celebrity's favorite dish. As Stewart reminisced, Hawes tapped away at a typewriter, noting where to insert a recipe from Martha's collection. In early 1981 they presented the finished manuscript to the publisher. Andy even supplied hundreds of his own photographs taken at Turkey Hill, which made the ideal backdrop because it expressed Martha's values as a cook, homemaker, caterer, and hostess. The dedication read: "To Andy, my husband, for his encouragement, good nature, and support. To Alexis, my daughter, for patience. My father, for instilling in me a love for all things beautiful."

Clarkson Potter ordered an initial run of 25,000 copies at $35 apiece. Stewart thought the number of copies was too small, but her publisher, well aware that any potential purchaser could buy three cookbooks for the price of *Entertaining*, stuck to the original order.

Of course, the book was a sensation—and for a number of reasons.

First, it was physically unusual: big, beautiful, and eye-catching. "[The author has] a fine eye, a sense of theater, and a respect for both the physical beauty and the taste of food," said a reviewer for *Library Journal*. "A rich kid book but never a snobbish one, this is a treat for eye and palate." Second, the book read like a long, informal magazine article. A reviewer for the *Christian Science Monitor* wrote admiringly, "Mrs. Stewart's relaxed but organized approach to what many would consider a monumental event reflects her practiced ease as a hostess and professional caterer. Her friendly, expressive form of party-giving is explained in [this book.]."

Unfortunately, references to the fine writing added to Elizabeth Hawes' feelings of being slighted. When the galley proofs—the first set of typeset pages—were distributed, Hawes saw that *Entertaining* was "by Martha Stewart," and "Text with Elizabeth Hawes" had been printed in smaller type. Hawes complained, but Stewart insisted on top billing and the editorial power. That's how things stayed.

But there were a few sour notes when the completed book went into stores, too, the most serious being charges of plagiarism.

Newsweek magazine said at least two recipes had already appeared in Julia Child's *Mastering the Art of French Cooking*. A photographer who had done some earlier magazine work for Martha Stewart also recognized shots of his, but they had been printed without permission and without compensation. However, the angriest accusations were raised by Barbara Tropp, author of the *Modern Art of Chinese Cooking*, for sale in bookstores at the same time as *Entertaining*. She identified a number of recipes that she said belonged to her. Stewart countered—with legal and publishing advice from Andy—that recipes circulated widely and were not owned. Still, Martha promised in future editions to give credit where it was due.

In any event, within two years *Entertaining* would be in its 14th printing, selling 11 times the number of copies printed for the initial run, for a total of 270,000—making it a huge best-seller in the formerly humble field of cookbook publishing. To date, *Entertaining* has gone into 30 printings, with more than 500,000 copies sold.

There was some controversy when "Entertaining" was released over whether or not some of the recipes were actually from Julia Child's cookbooks. Either way, the mistress of French cooking later appeared on Martha's television program and, together, they baked a European Christmas dessert. Both women labor to make such exotic fare a part of every family's cooking repertoire.

MARTHA
STEWART'S
HORS D'OEUVRES
HANDBOOK

PHOTOGRAPHS BY DANA GALLAGHER

The creation of Martha's fourteenth book, this hors d'oeuvres handbook in 1999, followed a set pattern of menu selection, setting selection, recipe writing, preparation, and photographing, and text writing. The books cost twice as much as other cooking titles, but the formula has proven successful. Martha is actually not interested in writing, instead she hires either a freelance or staff employees to do the writing for her.

5

SINGLE AND "LIVING"

I don't do anything unless I think it's going to be good; I'm real picky about that.

—Martha Stewart

With readers snapping up *Entertaining* despite the steep price, Martha Stewart worked closely with her publisher to get additional titles into bookstores as quickly as possible. Within a year *Martha Stewart's Quick Cook* (1983) appeared, followed by *Martha Stewart's Hors d'Oeuvres* (1984). Each book aimed at meeting the standard set by *Entertaining:* provide lots of information and creativity in a handsome package.

Book critics felt the new books met that standard. One reviewer wrote about *Martha Stewart's Hors d'Oeuvres*, "Virtually everything that can possibly be stuffed, skewered, layered, filled, spread, rolled, or dipped has been dressed for company in [this book]. This is no handbook on the order of something to tuck into your back pocket when you go birdwatching. It's an encyclopedia, a how-to compendium that will have you prowling the aisles of the supermarket, the crates at the farmstands, and the bins at the fancy markets to prepare for your next cocktail hour."

After the first few titles had been released, the process for creating a book with the Stewart style fell into a pattern. First Martha would select the menu of meals that came under the book's general theme— holiday entertaining, for instance, or easy dishes. Then the setting would be chosen. Healthy snacks might look best in outdoor environments like a walking trail, say, or beside a sunny swimming pool. Then the recipes would be written, and prepared examples from the menus would be photographed as if they were being served for a sit-down dinner or backyard summer party. At this point the book's art director would prepare a preliminary layout—an arrangement of the recipes and photographs on the pages. This is also when good decision-making would come in: Devote an entire page to a photograph of a cake whose color and texture is eye-catching? Or display it smaller on the page, surrounded by text?

The final step was writing the wraparound text itself—the informal, advice-filled story that guides the reader from one idea to the next, as if Martha herself was at the reader's shoulder. This step-by-step method resulted in books that all had a similar look and character. When creating a book about restoring an old home—Martha purchased another rundown 19th century Westport farmhouse and supervised its restoration—she took notes of what the builders did at each stage, and then displayed the story of the farmhouse coming back to life in words and pictures.

Having proved that food lovers would pay more than twice as much for books done in the Stewart style, Martha and her publisher brought out a new title almost every year: *Martha Stewart's Pies and*

Tarts (1985); *Weddings* (1987); *The Wedding Planner* (1988); *Martha Stewart's Quick Cook Menus* (1988); *Martha Stewart's Christmas* (1989); *Martha Stewart's Gardening Month by Month* (1991); *Martha Stewart's New Old House* (1992); *Martha Stewart's Menus for Entertaining* (1994); *The Martha Stewart Cookbook* (1995); *Martha Stewart's Healthy Quick Cook* (1997); *Martha Stewart's Hors d'Oeuvres Handbook* (1999). *Martha Stewart's Christmas* and *The Martha Stewart Cookbook* were both *New York Times* best-sellers.

The steady demand for the books, plus Stewart's galloping increase in popularity, led to yet another business: seminars on entertaining and decorating. For $900 to $1,200, participants could attend a three- or four-day seminar at Turkey Hill in groups of 20 or 30. After a light breakfast, students gathered in one of Martha's kitchens (the catering kitchen had been expanded to another building on the property) to watch and learn. Breaks in the schedule permitted attendees to explore the grounds and seek out the nearly 150 Araucana chickens that lay eggs in pastel colors. Because photographs of Martha's recipes usually featured Turkey Hill as the setting, many participants felt that the seminar fee was worth the price just to "step into" one of her books.

In November 1986 national television audiences, too, got the opportunity to peek into Martha's home when her first Thanksgiving Day special aired, showing her family making holiday preparations. The media routinely began referring to her as a tastemaker—someone whose influence was helping to shape people's opinions about fashion, decorating, and entertaining trends.

At that time Kmart, one of the country's largest discount department stores, also took notice. In 1986 Kmart the second only to Sears in size, but

Martha's first television program, a Thanksgiving Day special entitled, "Holiday Entertaining with Martha Stewart," aired on PBS in 1986. The success of the four books printed up to this point promised a significant television audience. Subsequent video projects helped her further break into a new media.

many of its stores had settled into a comfortable go-nowhere philosophy of serving customers who had to settle for rock-bottom prices. Moreover, the stores needed a facelift—something on the floor to brighten the aisles—to attract customers who were not only bargain hunters but style conscious, too. To Kmart executives, Martha Stewart seemed like the breath of fresh air that their stores could use.

She was receptive to the idea and probably encouraged because the retail giant had already enlisted another celebrity for its promotional push. In August 1985 Jaclyn Smith, star of the 1970s

Charlie's Angels television show and a fixture of 1980s miniseries, had introduced her own line of "value conscious" sportswear apparel in Kmart stores. Kmart executives held out the possibility to Martha that their organization could serve as the springboard for an expanded line of Martha Stewart products, too.

Stewart agreed to a five-year contract for $200,000 a year, plus $3,000 per store visit (she was required to make 30 a year), and a number of other financial incentives. The deal would not be made public until 1987, giving her time to create a line of special Dutch Boy paint colors and Martha Stewart bed linens and towels.

In the meantime, though, Stewart grew frustrated with the terms of her contract and what she later called "quality control" problems with her inventory. "When I first started with Kmart, I was very enthusiastic to build a fine business with them," she said later. "Little did I know that management was extremely weak and their inventory control and computer programs a complete disaster." The relationship with Kmart fizzled, and in hindsight it may have been one of the first signs that Martha needed someone to handle the strictly business side of what was now legally known as Martha Stewart, Inc.

In any case, even more projects beckoned. In 1988 Crown Publishers produced a series of four videos, *Martha Stewart's Secrets of Entertaining*, building on the success of one of her most popular books, *Weddings*, published in 1987.

The word "secrets" in the title of the video series is really no exaggeration. One of the primary appeals of her books—and *Weddings* is a good example—is the generous amount of detail and insider advice. In a reassuring voice, *Weddings* offers secrets that only an experienced hostess and caterer would know. For example, in a section about how to determine the number of serving portions, Stewart tips off the reader: "[I]n the course of my ten years of catering, I have also learned that there are simple rules based on simple mathematics that help make a party perfect. . . . [F]or a cocktail party reception, ten to twelve different hors d'oeurves with two or three of each per person and three or four drinks each is about right, but if an elaborate dinner is in the wings, a variety of five or six light hors d'oeuvres with three to five per person will suffice. At small dinners, with plate service, I portion-cook, a restaurant method in which each guest is allotted, say, a given number of asparagus stalks and a single steak." This kind of tested information is invaluable to brides planning their weddings—and naturally helped to make the book a success, even at $50 a copy, in 1987. However, with the publication of *Weddings*, another secret emerged that Stewart was not happy to reveal: her own marriage was ending.

While she was away promoting the new book, Andy moved out of their house and into an apartment. In a case of ill-timed irony, Martha had included in *Weddings* her memories of the day she and Andy were married at the chapel on the campus of Columbia University almost 27 years earlier. She described the music that Andy had selected (Pachelbel's "Canon in D Major"), the flowers she carried, and the simple lunch for the family at a hotel not far from the chapel. Now in the course of making recommendations as a wedding planner, she also had to plan for a future as an unmarried woman. In 1988 Andy filed for divorce.

Later, reflecting on the reasons for his leaving, Martha said, "I noticed him growing away, but I didn't pay any attention to it. He said I was too much for him, that I was going too far too fast. . . . If I should be punished for being too critical or too perfectionist, I've been punished."

Over the next two years, she poured her attention

and energy into a slew of projects. *The Wedding Planner* (1988) followed on the heels of *Weddings*. The following year, *Martha Stewart's Christmas*, filled with pictures of family members celebrating the holidays at Turkey Hill, rocketed to the number-one nonfiction best-seller on the *New York Times* list. In partnership with CBS, she consulted on *Dinner for Two* and *Breakfast in Bed*, collections of music designed to provide atmosphere for the menus and recipes she chose that accompanied each CD or cassette in the series.

And then, with the entrepreneurial knack to not only sense a need in the marketplace but also think of a profitable idea for answering it, Martha struck out in a new direction: planning a magazine.

It was clear to Martha that many women wanted to do home-centered things. Still, there were hints of a public backlash developing against Martha and her success. As Patricia McLaughlin wrote in a *New York Times Magazine* article about women wanting to be like Martha Stewart:

> Lots of women, especially women with children and jobs, already have too much to do and nowhere near enough time to do it. You see them zoned out in their rare moments of forced idleness at stoplights or in the check-out line, clicking through the agendas in their heads—8 o'clock meeting, plumber, grass seed, groceries, dry cleaner. . . .

On the other hand, an upbeat, breezy Martha Stewart magazine—filled with seasonal tips about getting organized for spring, or about devoting just an hour to work on a creative project—might fill the gap in busy women's lives in a way no decorating guide or cookbook could.

Stewart floated her idea before S. I. Newhouse, owner of the magazine publishing empire Advance Publications, Inc., which counted among its properties

The New Yorker, Self, Vogue, Glamour, and *House & Garden*. But he didn't like the concept, saying, "If I gave you a magazine with your name on it, I'd have to let Anna [Wintour, editor of *Vogue*] call it *Anna Winter's Vogue*." She then met with mass-media giant Rupert Murdoch, whose empire spans continents. His response: an unequivocal "No."

But the newly-merged Time Warner company was in a mood to take creative risks. Executives there offered Stewart the chance to produce two test issues. If they sold well, then Time Warner would move to the next step: deciding whether to launch *Martha Stewart Living*, as the magazine would be called, either monthly or every two months.

Like a starting gun being fired, creating an entirely new magazine set off a scramble for Martha and her staff. Working out of vacant offices at the Time Warner building, a bevy of writers, editors, photographers, and layout designers—many of them hired on short notice—hurried to meet the November deadline. One short-term staffer recalls the pressures and confusion:

> The woman who hired people to work on the maiden issue of *Martha Stewart Living* was widely known to have prefaced her job offers with the phrase, "Would you rather work for Martha Stewart or be boiled in oil?" . . . I met Martha exactly once, when she looked into the small borrowed office in which I was inputting her launch party guest list onto a Mac, squinted, and said "Who are you?"

Nevertheless, when the first issue of *Martha Stewart Living* appeared in July 1991, a quarter-million copies flew off the newsstands. A repeat success with the second issue convinced Time Warner that the magazine was a winner. Stewart signed to produce the magazine as a monthly publication for an annual salary of $400,000, plus an expense account as well as cash bonuses as the magazine's circulation and advertising

Despite being rejected by two publishing companies, the magazine Martha Stewart Living *was first printed in 1991 and 250,000 copies sold quickly. The main topics covered include home decorating, cooking and entertaining, gardening, crafts, holidays, household organization, and weddings. By 1998, 2.1 million copies were selling. Special issues, such as "Clotheskeeping," also appeared.*

accounts increased. Acquiring a large and devoted audience in its seven years of existence, the magazine has increased its readership to 2.1 million. Currently *Martha Stewart Living* is published ten times a year, and *Martha Stewart Weddings*—"a complete guide to wedding planning"—comes out quarterly.

Each issue of *Martha Stewart Living* opens with "A Letter from Martha," which comments on one or more topics in that issue. But "Remembering," her essay that appears as the last page in each issue, is really Stewart's "opportunity to flex her literary muscles on a wistful subject of her choosing," as Kate Moses, a writer for the e-zine *Salon.com*, puts it. The essay is usually very personal, often recalling scenes from her childhood and often rather revealing, whether Stewart means to be or not. For example, her "Remembering" essay for the special Halloween issue in 2000 began:

> My mother and father were not unlike other parents in our Nutley neighborhood when it came to Halloween. Dad was an excellent conceptualist and visionary: He always came up with the costume themes, knowing which of his six children would make a great pirate, matador, clown, or flapper.

If there were any doubt that Eddie Kostyra was infuriatingly bossy and controlling, this thumbnail description seems to confirm it. After all, how many parents decide in advance what their children are going to be for Halloween? Said Moses, "I've often wondered why someone doesn't pull the plug on 'Remembering' before she really embarrasses herself."

The rest of the magazine regularly features how-to information about seven core areas—Home, Cooking & Entertaining, Gardening, Crafts, Holidays, Keeping, and Weddings. But the tone and outlook of the magazine can't be reduced to a formula or even a tried-and-true format of seven dependable sections. Its appeal has more to do with the way that Stewart's magazine makes readers feel.

Patricia McLaughlin, in her *New York Times Magazine* article, put her finger on the key reason for the success of *Martha Stewart Living*:

> To its two million readers, most of them managers and professionals, her magazine presents the prospect of coming home to something more pleasant than ambient mess and frozen fish sticks. It offers opportunities to do something right for a change—whether it's building a window box or baking a loaf of eight-grain bread—without compromises, memos, and budget constraints.

Within a few years Stewart would find a partner in
another entrepreneurial woman, who would make use
of that special feeling Stewart followers had and create
a distinctive brand of marketing that said "Martha
Stewart" all over it.

Martha was named one of "America's 25 Most Influential People" in 1996 by Time Magazine *for becoming an important role model with her ubiquitous home-related advice and suggestions. Parodies and criticisms always erupt after receiving such a title, people either loved her or hated her. Still, there is no denying she has become a major force in popular culture.*

6

TELEVISION TO
TIME MAGAZINE

Martha really demands perfection, and she attracts people who are like her.

—Sharon L. Patrick, president of Martha Stewart Living Omnimedia

By 1993 Martha Stewart had 3 million books in print. With that kind of name recognition, it was a natural development in her career to tackle the television market.

The power of daytime television to promote cooking, crafts, and hobby shows is legendary. Famous chefs such as Jeff Smith, Graham Kerr, and Julia Child all began in small viewer markets, then gradually gained national audiences, creating a huge market for their books and products. Knowing this, Stewart eagerly accepted invitations to appear on the NBC network beginning in 1991. Every other Wednesday morning, the *Today* show aired a segment of *Martha Stewart Living* magazine, hosted by Martha, who presented how-to ideas about gardening, kitchen projects, or decorating, for instance.

In 1993 CBS recognized a "good thing"—one of Stewart's

favorite phrases—in viewer responses to Martha's relaxed style before the cameras and offered her a weekly syndicated television program. As *Salon.com* writer Mary Elizabeth Williams pointed out in "She's Martha and You're Not," "For all her recipes, tips and advice, the main thing that Martha offers to her public is herself, her cool, well-assembled exterior." The 30-minute program, *Martha Stewart Living,* aired at 8:30 A.M. on Sunday mornings throughout the country.

The show introduced itself each Sunday morning with chirpy wake-up music and a preview montage of Martha involved in gardening, cooking, decorating, or taking field trips to interesting places—four general topics that resembled the format of the magazine. The viewing audience was smitten with the show's pleasantness, with all of the scenes washed in sunlight and bright colors.

Its impact on viewers was enormous. When she did a guacamole-making segment with New York City restaurateur Josefina Howard, for instance, lines soon formed around the block at Howard's Rosa Mexicana eatery. *Entertainment Weekly* magazine dubbed the program "television's best weekend getaway." It ran weekly for four seasons between 1993 and 1997 on the CBS network and received three Daytime Emmy Awards.

The same year that her TV show began, another event decisively influenced Martha Stewart's life, one that would ultimately change the helter-skelter nature of her various ventures—the books, the magazine, the videos, the television program—into one focused business entity: Martha Stewart Living Omnimedia (MSLO).

During a week-long climb up 19,340-foot Mt. Kilimanjaro in Tanzania, Martha met fifty-year-old Sharon Patrick. A graduate of Harvard's Master of Business Administration (MBA) program, Patrick was finishing a year-long hiatus from 9–5 investment management work, instead "undertaking entrepreneurial business ventures with ideas and people that interested me," she has explained. Martha Stewart was among the group of climbers. Patrick noticed that Martha didn't want to wear standard-issue hiking gear. "[Her outfit] was bright green, bright red, bright yellow. Martha expected to look like [the movie] *Out of Africa*. I didn't care what I wore. That's the difference between Martha and me." Stewart eventually changed into a khaki-colored outfit, which camouflaged her so well that she became separated from the group. When everyone joined up again, Patrick and Stewart fell into step figuratively as well as literally, discussing how they could unite Martha's many business ventures into one corporate "brand."

"Martha fell in love with Sharon's mind," said Charlotte Beers, chairman emeritus of Ogilvy & Mather Worldwide Inc. and a mutual friend. By the time they came back down from the top of Kilimanjaro a few days later, they had roughed out key points of a new business plan.

The problem, as Patrick saw it, was that Stewart's businesses and contracts were too disjointed.

> When I met Martha she had various fragmented businesses and business arrangements. Some were hers, independently, and some were partnerships with others, like Time Warner. Martha had lots of ideas and a great sense of the possibilities of the businesses. . . . Conversely, I had a lot of ideas about multimedia. So we started to build MSLO, which combined all of Martha's business interests into a single, integrated, synergistic company.

Sharon Patrick, it should be noted, is not a Martha-wannabe. Single and living in a penthouse on Manhattan's Upper East Side, the San Diego native likes to garden on her sprawling terrace, play baseball, and scuba dive, but she doesn't share many of Stewart's personal interests. (At one festive event where Martha was sipping a glass of turquoise champagne that matched her outfit, Stewart asked her friend and business partner, "Doesn't this remind you of the blue skin of a scarab beetle, Sharon?" To which Patrick laughed. "Martha, how am I supposed to know what a scarab beetle looks like?") Patrick's specialty is finding the potential in businesses to make them stronger—run better and more profitably.

Those skills had earlier been put to the test in 1990, when Cablevision Systems Corp. chief executive Charles F. Dolan appointed Sharon Patrick president of his struggling programming division, Rainbow Programming Holdings Inc. "She has a great power to analyze and organize," Dolan recalled. At Rainbow, Patrick added new programs, got rid of the deadwood, and increased the company's revenues by 50 percent. When her three-year $325,000-a-year contract expired, she left. As she explained, "I'm a startup and a turnaround person. When a job's done, it's done."

Now, with Martha Stewart, Patrick saw an opportunity to do what she had been "yearning" to do for years: create a brand in all areas of media— publishing, the Internet, radio, and television—a true omnimedia company. ("I always thought it was good economics and the wave of the future," she once said.) However, before this goal was met, the company had to become a much more streamlined organization.

The challenge was huge. Martha's empire entailed 13 books, the 10-issues-a-year magazine, the daily 90-second radio spots, the daily syndicated television show, weekly television appearances, the syndicated weekly newspaper column, the prime-time specials, the Martha by Mail direct-mail catalog, the Internet website and the K-mart, Sherwin-Williams, and Sears retail partnerships. In addition to the Time Warner publishing ventures, Stewart had dozens of other deals for additional books, television shows, and new product lines. The company was so scattered and inefficient that 10 banks refused to consider lending Patrick and Stewart money for creating MSLO.

To manage all this activity under the MSLO umbrella, Sharon Patrick had to urge a rather reluctant Martha Stewart to design a traditional-looking organization management chart of lines and boxes, showing who was responsible for what. As Stewart told an audience of business students and faculty at Columbia University, "I knew we needed one, but I hate the look of those things. I have box phobia." So Stewart created an organizational "tree," instead, with each employee represented by a leaf whose color is one of the 40 Stewart-approved colors that appear throughout Marthaland, even in the corporate offices. Initially Stewart asked each person on the staff to decide what leaf he or she wanted to be. But Patrick quickly corrected her: "No, Martha. You assign the leaves." Stewart chose a beech leaf for herself, she remembered, "because it's the mother of all trees."

In the meantime, Stewart's business continued to grow in several directions at once. In June 1995 reruns of the show began airing five mornings a week on cable television's Lifetime channel. By then five million viewers were watching in 84 percent of the nation's viewing markets. On the newsstands *Martha Stewart Living* was selling approximately a half-million copies every issue. The *New York Times* syndicate picked up her newspaper column *askMartha*. (Within a few years 230 newspapers in the United States and Canada would be carrying it.) In light of all the activity surrounding her business ventures, Time Warner created a new corporation, Martha Stewart Living Enterprises, in partnership with Stewart as chairman and chief executive officer.

And if that wasn't enough, she had her television specials.

In December 1995 Martha visited the White House and interviewed First Lady Hillary Rodham Clinton. In the course of the interview, Stewart spoke with Mrs. Clinton about the holiday preparations at the White House, noting that every year it is adorned with decorations from all over the country. The interview provided the inspiration for *Great American Wreaths* (1996) by Martha Stewart, showing readers how to create a wreath for every state. The chapters explain different wreath-making methods: applying dried materials to wire-wreath forms; filling forms with soil for living wreaths; and gathering prairie grasses, swags of evergreens, and even a giant tumbleweed into wreaths. The last wreath in the book is an oak-leaf-and-gilded-acorn creation that Martha and the First Lady hung on the iron balustrade of the South Portico of the White House.

It was a far-flung empire—one that needed steady supervision. By late 1995 Patrick was practically living at Turkey Hill. "I was working through the night around the kitchen table, trying to figure out how to pull her empire together."

At the height of the Martha Stewart media tidal wave in 1996, *Time* magazine named Martha Stewart one of "America's 25 Most Influential People."

Finally in February 1997, after a great deal of negotiating, Sharon Patrick "pulled off the buyout" of Martha Stewart Living Enterprises from Time Warner, turning "America's favorite hostess" into a full-blown corporation 15 years after she had first put her toe in the media waters by publishing

"Home for the Holidays" on CBS network with muppet, Miss Piggy. Martha started doing regular television appearances in 1991 with short segments airing every other week on NBC. CBS then offered her a national, weekly 30-minute show in 1993. Spots on "CBS This Morning" and periodic prime-time specials eventually followed.

Entertaining. "Sharon is great at bringing warring parties together," said Joseph Ripp, Time's chief financial officer. "Without Sharon, there would have been no deal."

For $75 million Time agreed to sell more than 80 percent of its investment in Martha Stewart Living Enterprises, now renamed Martha Stewart Living Omnimedia. Also, as part of an expanding CBS partnership, Martha Stewart began an exclusive affiliation with *CBS This Morning*—now renamed *The Early Show*. The television segments include the *Martha Stewart Living* syndicated series, weekly *Early Show* appearances, and periodic CBS prime-time specials, all in partnership with divisions of CBS Television.

Then two weeks after hammering down the Time Warner buyout, Patrick scored yet another victory by renegotiating Stewart's contract with Kmart.

Despite how that relationship had been limping along for nine years, Patrick persuaded Kmart to put "Martha's World" boutiques in prime store space. In return, Kmart got Stewart's signature on bed and bath linens in the colors "she detests": burgundy and hunter green. According to Steve Riman, a Kmart vice-president, "Sharon helped me convince Martha that this is what the mass market wants." To sweeten the deal on Martha's side, Sharon Patrick got $16 million up front from Kmart and a percentage of the profits on every paint can and pillowcase sold.

And Martha personally keeps an eye on her empire. Stacy Perman of *Time* magazine reported not long after the Kmart deal went through,

> there she was . . . rolling a cart down the aisle at the Linden, New Jersey, [Kmart]. With one hand on her cart, the other on her cellular phone, multitask Martha snapped up $330 worth of her own line and . . . helped a customer pick out a bridal-shower gift, signed an autograph, and expressed dismay when her favorite-color sheets (light aqua) were obscured by a steel column.

The most recent media, the internet and world wide web, was Martha's next project. Her company's website, marthastewart.com, combines information on 24-hour bulletin boards and live chat sessions with experts, along with, of course, merchandising opportunities. It may prove to be the best vehicle yet for promoting Martha's vision of living comfortable yet stylishly.

When a startled shopper spied Stewart and remarked, "I wonder what she's doing here," his companion replied, "She owns it."

That's not true, of course, but "Martha's World" does account for most of Kmart's home department sales.

Later that year, on September 8, 1997, *Martha Stewart Living* became a daily program. The same day, Westwood One Entertainment launched *askMartha* as a 90-second daily radio feature, and *marthastewart.com* appeared on the Internet.

Within a month the website had averaged 550,000 visitors a week. (By comparison, that same year *National Geographic*'s site was getting 500,000 visitors a month.) The site sends daily reminders on a variety of topics and enables users to shop the Martha Stewart online catalog. In addition, seven distinct channels—Home, Cooking & Entertaining, Gardening, Crafts, Holidays, Keeping, and Weddings—each offer live discussion forums every weekday from 2 P.M. to midnight; 24-hour bulletin boards where visitors can post advice, queries, and replies; and weekly live question-and-answer sessions with in-house and guest experts. Stewart believed it was a sure-fire plan: "Say our audience is 20 million people. Over the next four years, if each one has a computer and spends $1,000 on our online system, even over five years, even on software products, it is the hugest business. Do the math."

Today, Stewart and Patrick remain close friends. As their mutual friend Charlotte Beers said, "Sharon is not easily daunted. They are very loyal to each other." The two often spend weekends at Stewart's East Hampton home and travel the world mixing work with play. At the offices of MSLO, decorated in blond wood under bright lights, Patrick and Stewart work in the same room, head-to-head at antique French post-master's desks. All around them 160 people create the recipes, gardening tips, and housekeeping advice that Stewart shares with millions of readers, listeners, and viewers. In addition to relying on her army of decorating experts, Stewart finds help from family members. Her mom and her sisters occasionally show up in the pages of *Martha Stewart Living* or on her television show.

Although Stewart is in charge of the company as its chairperson and chief executive officer, as president Patrick is said to be demanding and known for her full-speed-ahead attitude. "Sure I'm demanding," she said. "But so are [IBM chairman] Lou Gerstner and [former Chrysler Corporation chairman] Lee Iacocca. If I were a man, I'd be called a great leader."

But at least one person watching from the wings wasn't impressed by Stewart's success. Jerry Oppenheimer, author of several tell-all biographies of celebrities, deliberately set out to debunk what he said was the Martha Stewart myth. In 1997, the year Martha Stewart Living Omnimedia was created, bookstores came out with Oppenheimer's 400-page *Martha Stewart—Just Desserts: The Unauthorized Biography.*

Martha was said to be furious.

Winemaker, Gina Gallo, with Martha on "Martha Stewart Living" television
show. The Food Network was her next foray into television with 14 half-hour
appearances a week, made up mostly of previously-taped food segments from
the MSL show.

7

JUST DESSERTS TO SHARES

The subject matter that I am really spending my time on has become an acceptable subject matter.

—Martha Stewart

"She's all about these nostalgic reminiscences about cooking and food and family life," Jerry Oppenheimer said in an interview about *Just Desserts*, his tell-all biography of Martha Stewart. "She presents herself as the perfect mother, the perfect cook, the perfect housewife. I've gone back and proven that's all myth. Martha's not the doyenne of domesticity, but more like Betty Crocker From Hell."

Oppenheimer, who had previously penned raunchy profiles of Rock Hudson, Barbara Walters, and Ethel Kennedy, interviewed 400 of Martha's friends and family to dig up everything he could about her childhood, marriage, catering days, and divorce. "While some people call Oppenheimer a mean-spirited mudslinger, most admit that he did extensive research before writing this explosive investigative biography," wrote one reviewer.

Calling Oppenheimer mean-spirited is no under-statement. He painted Stewart as an ambitious phony who grew up "with a cold mother, an abusive father, and white-bread sandwiches in place of gourmet meals" and portrayed her as a miser who salvaged food from one catering job to use at the next and drained "half-empty wine glasses into vinegar gift bottles."

And Oppenheimer couldn't resist dramatizing horror stories about her temper. He details:

> When a new assistant cook snapped a knife blade while boning a leg of lamb, fear gripped the rest of the kitchen crew, who knew how violently Martha reacted when one of her implements was broken or damaged and had to be replaced. The kitchen supervisor turned ashen and told the frightened offender, "Just take the blade and bury it in the trash. Don't mention this to anyone. For your sake, forget it ever happened."

Judging by the reaction of some people who know Stewart, Oppenheimer's book must have in many ways rung true. An employee at the bookstore near Martha's Connecticut estate, Turkey Hill, gushed about her enthusiasm for the book: "Isn't it delicious? It's salacious!"

Although angered by the book, Stewart didn't try to disprove the tales but merely dismissed it instead as a "hideous piece of yellow journalism."

"All I do," said Stewart in her own defense, is "write cookbooks and teach people how to do good things."

Criticizing and poking fun at Stewart is not new. A *New York Times Magazine* article details how *Newsweek* called her "perfectly perfect," then mocked how "on a typical morning, she's already fed the chickens, built a tool shed and launched a new business by the time the rest of us are stumbling into the shower." The *New Republic* magazine couldn't resist making fun of her for owning too many gardening tools. And author Tom Connor wrote three parodies of Stewart's entertaining tips, which were advertised as "only slightly more impossible than the Hospitality Guru's own projects," but which sold well. They were *Is Martha Stewart Living?* (1995), *Martha Stewart's Better Than You at Entertaining* (1996), and *Martha Stewart's Excruciatingly Perfect Weddings* (1998).

To people in the food world, however, barbs aimed at Martha Stewart are old hat, according to Lisa Ekus, head of a publicity company representing cookbook authors and chefs, who was interviewed by *New York* magazine when *Just Desserts* came out. "I don't think it's going to be any surprise. Her life has been quite public. . . . People are going to continue to aspire to be Martha. She spins a fantasy and she spins it beautifully." Then she added, "We're all scooping out cabbage to put dip in it because of Martha. That's not going to change if she's nicer or meaner."

Stewart tries to exhibit a sense of humor about her I-can-do-anything-better-than-you reputation. She has appeared in American Express commercials in which she expertly tiles her swimming pool with cut up discarded credit cards. She's been on David Letterman's late-night show, responding in kind to his wisecracks. She even appeared at the MTV Music Awards with Busta Rhymes, smiling primly and seeming to enjoy looking oddly out of place as the Queen of Clean, standing beside a bemused tatooed rapper.

In any case, Stewart says she finds the criticism boring: "It's sexist, jealous, and stupid, and it all comes from one little area—journalism."

Journalism, however, is also quick to trumpet her latest successes. On October 19, 1999, Martha Stewart Living Omnimedia became a publicly traded stock on the New York Stock Exchange. (When a stock becomes "public," it is available to anyone who wants to purchase it and invest in the company.) Business writers covered the offering as a major event. *ABC News.com*'s online website *The Street.com* carried a

Ever unpredictable and ground breaking, Martha joined rap artist Busta Ryhmes to present an award on MTV's Music Awards Show in 1997. She has a sense of humor about her public persona and has made commercials poking fun of herself, and even did a cameo on the sitcom Ellen *with comedienne Ellen Degeneres, where Martha revealed the joys of "ordering out."*

photograph of Stewart outside the exchange with the caption: "Martha Stewart, chairman and CEO [chief executive officer] of Martha Stewart Omnimedia's red hot initial public offering, leads this week's IPO [initial public offering] hopefuls."

Earlier that year, in July, Martha and Sharon Patrick had filed the paperwork that is the first step in the complicated process of offering stock to the public. They were banking on getting about $42 million of the proceeds from selling stock so that they could buy out Time's remaining 20 percent of MSLO.

Although 21 companies offered stock for the first time that day, stock watchers were betting on big sales for just two—MSLO and the World Wrestling Federation. Beth Kwon, writing for *The Street.com*, reported:

> Wall Street embraced both ventures. Shares in Martha Stewart nearly tripled at the outset on the New York Stock Exchange, before giving up a little of its gains. . . .
>
> Martha Stewart Living shares were priced late Monday at $18, at the top of the revised $16-to-$18 range announced earlier in the day. The shares initially had been expected to sell in a range of $13 to $15.
>
> The stock opened at $37.25 a share, soared to $52, and was trading at $37.81-1/4 Tuesday afternoon. The stock closed at 35 1/2.

In one day, MSLO had sold 7.2 million shares of common stock. Already the company had reported earning $14.2 in net income in the months ending June 30. But with the price of the stock tripling in one day—totaling approximately $260 million—Martha Stewart became one of the wealthiest women in the United States.

In fact, 1999 was a very good year for Martha Stewart and MSLO overall. The television show doubled in length from 30 minutes to one hour; the new format allowed for a number of additional and extended features, including an "askMartha" segment that let viewers have their phone calls and e-mails answered by Martha on the air, plus "more regional coverage, including segments on local gardening and entertaining, ethnic cooking, and regional crafts." Also, the Food Network cable channel began airing a half-hour program twice a day, seven days a week, consisting mainly of food-related segments from previous *Martha Stewart Living* television programs.

As of 2001, over 90 percent of U.S. television households could see *Martha Stewart Living* six days a week, primarily between 9 A.M. and noon. The show is taped in "state-of-the-art" studios in Westport and

East Hampton. In the $4 million Westport studio, white marble countertops and a marble-topped dining table in the kitchen set off Martha's collections of green and turquoise dishes, including restaurant ware in her favorite milky green. The set also includes a craft room and a mudroom, where people can remove their dirty shoes.

The East Hampton studio is based on the kitchen in her East Hampton house. Cherry-stained cabinets and dark-gray soapstone countertops complement Stewart's collections of copper pots and pans, yellow ware, and brown transfer ware. Besides the kitchen, the East Hampton set has a mudroom, a pantry, a home-office space, and a library.

The format of the show, like the magazine, devotes segments to a handful of core topics: Gardening, Restoring, Entertaining, Good Things, Decorating, Cooking, Collecting, Crafts, Field Trips, and Home-keeping. Stewart also welcomes expert guests, including chefs, gardeners, and artisans, to explain such things as "making a duvet [comforter] cover to preparing a traditional Argentinean barbecue to learning about the history of Wedgwood china." Out-of-studio excursions are also a regular part of the program, and one season presented such disparate activities as learning roping techniques on a Colorado dude ranch, making wine in the Napa Valley, and spending a day with a Maine lobsterman.

The program has received many honors for its efforts. Since its debut *Martha Stewart Living* has received a total of 16 Emmy nominations, for both the show and its host, and in May 1998 the show received the James Beard Foundation Award for the Best National Cooking Segment.

By 2001, MSLO had achieved the integrated business strategy that Martha Stewart and Sharon Patrick had hoped to achieve by combining all of Martha Stewart under one roof. The television show, the

Martha's colleague, Sharon Patrick (right), managed the buyout of Martha Stewart Living Enterprises from Time Inc. in 1997, making it an independent corporation. To raise more money to complete the purchase, the company first offered shares of its stock for public purchase on October 19, 1999. Here, Martha rings the opening bell for the day's trading on the New York Stock Exchange with Sharon and NYSE President, William Johnson (left).

magazine, the website, "Martha's World" at Kmart, and millions of Martha by Mail catalogs all promote Martha Stewart products while maintaining Stewart as America's leading tastemaker. "Marthaland is a one-stop shop," as Stacy Perman wrote, "for everything from bed to kitchen to garden, where one thing stylishly builds on another."

There was really only one problem: Martha was no longer happy in Westport, Connecticut, where it all started.

Westport, CT, her home of 28 years, had changed too much for Martha. Or was it Martha that had changed too much for Westport? After a rather bitter departure from the town in 2000, she purchased several properties in Westchester County, NY, reforming a previously divided estate. She had a new house and grounds to renovate and rehabilitate, and perhaps more importantly, new neighbors.

8

FROM WESTPORT TO WESTCHESTER COUNTY

I think baking cookies is equal to Queen Victoria running an empire.
There's no difference in how seriously you take the job, how seriously you
approach your whole life.

—Martha Stewart

The headline introducing a piece that appeared in a Sunday issue of the *New York Times Magazine* in early April 2000 read "Martha Stewart Leaving." Underneath was Stewart's essay, which she had titled "Why I'm Getting Out of Westport."

To the readers of *Martha Stewart Living*, the style was familiar. The first-person essay sounded like one of her "Remembering" pieces at the end of the magazine. But this time there was an unmistakable tone of regret. She began:

> I have tried very hard not to move. I've been a resident of Westport, Conn., for almost three decades—28 years—and it makes me sad just to think about leaving my beloved Turkey Hill house. But this town, as beautiful as it is, just doesn't work for me any longer. So I've decided to pack up for someplace new.

To the viewers of her television show who had spent countless hours watching her in her Turkey Hill kitchen—preparing for holidays, welcoming friends and guests, sharing tips about making a dish in her style that's both intimate and teacher-like at the same time—it must have seemed unthinkable that Stewart would want to be anywhere else except in the center of Marthaland. After all, that's where her admirers wanted to be.

But Stewart said there had been "warning signs" for some time, which she had tried to ignore by focusing on giving her home a fresh look:

> The rooms were painted using an entirely new and beautiful palette of colors. The furniture was carefully edited, and the cupboards were rearranged so that only the nicest things remained. I increased my menagerie of pets, adding two more kittens to the six I already cherished. I started keeping chinchillas as pets; they now number seven. The already bountiful gardens were enlarged, and more trees and shrubs and perennials were planted—all to entice me to stay here.

But the old magic of the place couldn't be recaptured, not the possibilities that existed when she, Andy, and Alexis had moved into the tumbledown 1805 house in the early 1970s. "[T]hings change," she said. "People change. And it's time for me to move on."

What had happened exactly?

She said she no longer felt like she belonged in Westport—she no longer even felt welcome. Westport was known as a community of artists, writers, and entrepreneurs who commuted to New York. But then, she said, "More people started to come into town than leave it every day. . . . Main Street's small-town character gradually altered—rents rose, squeezing out the old 'unconnected' businesses, and chain stores moved in, making it just like so many other 'shopping destination' towns."

Living in Westport had even more problems for Martha:

> My own entrepreneurial ventures caused me lots of pain and loss of friends in the neighborhood where I lived . . . my attempt to run a catering business from our basement created embarrassing conflicts that would not have existed if I had been a seamstress or an illustrator operating a business of similar size from home. . . . Even after I moved my business to a commercial space, some neighbors continued to make life difficult. I found that I began distancing myself from my neighbors, just as they had distanced themselves from me.

She tried to make friends with new neighbors by offering fresh eggs and garden produce, but on both occasions she only felt enmity from her neighbors (one time they even slammed a door on her!). "I no longer feel connected to the neighborhood, the neighbors or even the town," Martha said.

Apart from the changes that had taken place in Westport, in reading between the lines of her essay it's clear that being Martha Stewart carries a price. Commenting on why this might be, Sharon Patrick, president of Martha Stewart Living Omnimedia pointed out,

> First, she's a celebrity, and celebrities are often lightning rods. Second, the fact that she is focused on the home and hearth is sort of counterculture. She has the guts and the talent and the insight to take that on. People find her perfection maddening—they feel competitive, they feel jealous, they feel inadequate.

"Stewart's perfectionism, encyclopedic knowledge, and bottomless capacity for work were not universally admired," *Britannica. com* writer Anita Wolff wrote in an article reviewing the year 1995. "She was censured for setting an impossible model for harried working mothers, and her glorification of a home-centered existence seemed to some a step backward for women."

"She drives me insane," said Katherine Stuart, a Los Angles woman interviewed for a *Time* magazine piece with the headline "Attention K Martha Shoppers: Martha Stewart can decorate anything, and she rules a $150 million empire." Stuart explained, "Part of me loves her. I mean, my God, she picks her own eggs, makes her own paint and makes everything so pretty. I had a subscription for two months, but she made me feel so deficient, so I canceled. Reading it made me feel bad about myself."

Charlotte Beers, chairman emeritus of Ogilvy & Mather and a friend of Stewart's, calls her a "really elegant teacher," but also adds, "It's true she can make a pie in four minutes, and I'm a great piemaker myself. It's maddening."

But Stewart has a ready response to criticisms like these. If women feel in competition with her on the home front—even a women like Beers who made her mark in the uppermost ranks of business—it's because the Martha Stewart lifestyle speaks to a need. She explained in an interview:

> Women are wanting to spend more time at home, men are wanting to spend more time at home. They want to garden, they want to do all that stuff. And they want to see their kids grow up, and that's what's happened. That's why this intense interest in how to polish a floor, how to wash a car. You know, all that stuff is coming back.

If there's a conflict, it's in women themselves—not something created by Stewart, argued Patricia McLaughlin in a *New York Times Magazine* piece about Stewart titled "Public Enemy No.1." She wrote:

> Her audience is the last generation of Americans to have grown up with truly clean floors. And like Meg in *Little Women*, who found poverty harder to bear than her sisters because she remembered when they were rich, many of us are beginning to miss those clean floors and the other benefits of good housekeeping—order, beauty, comfort,

warmth. It's not that we want to go back (as if we had the choice). But, good as it is not to have to hang our whole identities on clean floors, it's also good to have them. And we haven't figured out how to have it both ways.

Mary Elizabeth Williams in her *Salon.com* piece, "She's Martha Stewart and You're Not" counters that trying to have it both ways is unrealistic and intimidating:

> For mere mortals who do not employ a staff of cooks, cleaners, pet experts, fashion coordinators, gift wrappers and chicken-coop cleaners, true Marthahood is impossible to maintain. While there's no doubt that even with one hand tied behind her back in a neat grosgrain ribbon, Martha could still bake, clean and throw together a hibiscus garland before breakfast, it doesn't change the daunting nature of the lifestyle she encourages.

On the other hand, perhaps there's a deeper issue in the debate too, writes novelist and social critic Joan

Skillfully transitioning to the boardroom, Martha attends a CEO summit with the other top executives from Microsoft, Alcoa Company, Dell Computer, Ford Motor Co., and Allied Signal, Inc. Her success has come not from writing every word, taking every photo in her publications, or making every sauce seen on television, but from having a vision of the larger picture that makes the overall package appeal to people.

Didion: women's reluctance to be as driven and committed to their own interests as men are. "The dreams and fears into which Martha Stewart taps are not of 'feminine' domesticity but of female power, of the woman who sits down at the table with the men and, still in her apron, walks away with the chips."

Said Stewart,

> I think baking cookies is equal to Queen Victoria running an empire. There's no difference in how seriously you take the job, how seriously you approach your whole life. That's why when people say, "Are you a feminist?" I say, "No, I'm not." I believe in a man and a woman being equal. I really believe that we can do anything we set our minds to. Sometimes that's a struggle; it's harder than it should be, and I think I have paid my dues. I certainly have worked extremely hard, and I've succeeded nicely.

Penn State University Professors Virginia Smith and Lynda Goldstein are working on *Reading Martha Stewart: It's a Good Thing*, a book tracing the ultimate homemaker's place in history as an advocate of American arts and crafts. "That's what Thomas Jefferson did with Monticello," Smith compares. "Ben Franklin had Martha's incredible notion of industry and frugality."

Looking back over her personal reasons for doing what she did, Stewart said, "I had a sense of what I needed as a woman, mother, housewife, homekeeper. And I used that as a basis for what I thought other people would need. A happy home. A beautiful garden. An edited landscape. I stand for a nice life with a pleasant environment, interspersed with business, with a love of art and music and all the other stuff. My trademark and I are the same. I stand for what I am."

But although standing for what she is has meant leaving the house in which she had lived for nearly three decades and decamping in November 2000 for a

It irritates some people that Martha, the ultimate home-maker, was reported to seldom provide dinner for her family even while working as a caterer. The deeper issues may be women's feelings of compe-tition or inadequacy next to someone who can "cook, clean, and start a new company before breakfast," and it may also be women's reluctance to pursue their own careers as fiercely as men.

new home, moving isn't that much of a hardship. The 153-acre estate she purchased in Bedford, New York, known as Cantitoe Corners, cost Stewart $15.6 million and dates back to the 1700s. The estate includes a 1784 farmhouse, a 1929 colonial-style winter house, and an 1897 teamster's cottage.

The editor-in-chief accepts a national Magazine Award for Martha Stewart Living's *photography in 1999. It's Martha's intention to "monopolize and influence" areas of communication. Her products and media outlets are doing well in 2001 despite stiff competition from numerous similar products and magazines and a downturn in the economy.*

9

LOOKING AHEAD

The year 2001 started strong for Martha Stewart Living Omnimedia (MSLO), with Stewart herself predicting continued growth for corporation. "Our expectation for another record year in 2001 is based upon solid growth catalysts," she declared.

That February the company announced the expansion of its *Martha Stewart Baby* publication from two issues per year to four. The two additional issues would comprise a new publication, *Martha Stewart Kids,* dedicated to the essentials of caring for a child from three to ten years of age. The plan was to alternate *Martha Stewart Baby* and *Martha Stewart Kids* every three months. *Martha Stewart Kids* would have a creative and educational focus, providing an array of ideas, activities, and projects that children can create on their own or with their parents.

Stewart said the company's aim of the four magazines was to attract and keep readers from young motherhood all the way through middle age:

Our monthly magazine, *Martha Stewart Living*, has become synonymous with trusted content for the home-maker. Our quarterly magazine, *Martha Stewart Weddings*, provides the bride-to-be with impeccable information and inspiration. With *Martha Stewart Baby* we now reach another demographic, those readers who need a different kind of content that will help make the nurturing, raising and education of young children a meaningful and fulfilling occupation. We apply our unique sense of style and substance to this most precious of subjects, and the result is a magazine full of wonderful ideas, necessary information and enchanting, simple projects.

MSLO also planned to increase the frequency *Martha Stewart Living*, from 11 to 12 times per year, by publishing an August issue and introducing a custom-published *Gardening* magazine that Kmart will mail to four million customers.

But magazine publishing is a rough-and-tumble business, and Stewart's four magazines have stiff competition on the newsstands. *Martha Stewart Living* battles for readers and advertising against such decorating, cooking, and lifestyle magazines as *Architectural Digest*, *Metropolitan Home*, *Bon Appetit*, *Food & Wine*, *Gourmet*, *O: The Oprah Magazine*, *Real Simple*, *Country Living*, *Better Homes & Gardens*, and *Southern Living*. *Martha Stewart Weddings* competes for the same readers and advertising dollars as *Bride's Magazine*, *Modern Bride*, *Bridal Guide*, and *Elegant Bride*. And both readers and advertisers are crucial to a magazine's success: the more readers a magazine can claim, the more advertisers will want to take out ad space in the magazine, and the more they can be charged for the ads.

Every three months corporations make financial status reports available to stockholders and the public, and when MSLO issued its first-quarter report for 2001, President and Chief Operating Officer Sharon

The Spring 2001 issue of Martha Stewart Baby. *The magazine, along with* Martha Stewart Living, *has been joined by other titles:* Weddings, *and* Kids. *The array of publications is meant to provide information for a woman through several stages of her life: as a bride-to-be, a homemaker, a mother of an infant, and as a mother of a toddler.*

Patrick attempted to gloss over some bad news that she had to deliver along with the good.

"While the advertising market has slowed, the Martha Stewart brand will provide strong growth for our company through 2001 and beyond. In fact, less than half of our revenue base is derived from advertising, as we have continued to grow and diversify our business mix," Patrick said.

In fact, because the corporation guaranteed their advertisers a minimum circulation of 2.15 million earlier in the year, up from 2.1 million in 2000, Patrick's statement and the report affected MSLO's performance on the stock market, as often happens when company's are forced to admit some kind of decline in business. The following day, the per-share price of MSLO stock dropped suddenly. As a result, the online business forecaster *Forbes.com* dubbed MSLO "Dog of the Day" after the market closed that day. Wall Street analysts, predicting a continued slow-down in MSLO's magazine revenues, doubted that the corporation's publications arm would be able to repeat its unusual success from 2000 in landing adver-tisers, when ad pages rose 17 percent that influenced a 22.5 percent increase in revenue from 1999.

Perhaps, then, it was more than coincidence when just about a month later, MSLO announced that the editor in chief of Martha Stewart Living, Stephen Drucker, would be leaving to "pursue new challenges"—the type of polite talk in business circles that usually masks a resignation or firing. Drucker was replaced by the man he himself had hired to assist him—again, a typical situation in business, where the next in charge moves up to replace the boss.

Drucker had recruited Douglas Brenner in 1999 to become *Martha Stewart Living*'s deputy editor. Brenner was promoted to executive editor in 2000. Before joining *Martha Stewart Living*, he had been the editor of *Garden Design*, a position he held for five years. Previously he had been executive editor of *Travel & Leisure* (1993–94), arts editor of *House & Garden* (1989–93), and executive editor of *Architec-tural Record* (1980–88). Brenner has also written about architecture and landscape design for the *New York Times* and the *(London) Times Literary Supple-ment,* and he was the recipient of the Garden Writers of America Award of Excellence for a 1996 feature article in *Garden Design.*

On other fronts besides *Martha Stewart Living*, it was full-speed ahead. In July 2000 MSLO worked with Rhino Entertainment Company to jointly produce and distribute a series of CDs that could accompany

MARTHA STEWART LIVING
home for the
holidays
SONGS TO GET YOU IN THE SPIRIT

The compact disk cover from one of Martha's music compilations suitable for specific holidays. The photo on the Halloween disk "Spooky Scary Sounds..." shows her sporting a beguiling black boa and yellow cat's eyes. Few CEOs have their own photo on almost every single product, as does Martha.

the magazines. *Martha Stewart Living*'s *Spooky Scary Sounds for Halloween,* a collection of sound effects for use at Halloween parties and for neighborhood trick-or-treaters, was released in September 2000, followed by *Martha Stewart Living: Home for the Holidays,* a compilation of traditional and contemporary holiday music. The year 2001 would likely see more CDs that touched on some of the favorite themes of the magazines.

And the newsstands would see special issues of MSLO magazines geared to holidays and the interests of readers. "In 2001, we intend to publish four special-interest publications consisting of content from our Baby and Kids core content area, one Holiday-themed special-interest publication, and one special interest publication focusing on technology," an official MSLO press release promised.

Chairman and CEO of Kmart, Charles Conawa, with Martha and two other celebrities that have lent their names to the retailer, Jaclyn Smith and Kathy Ireland, both actresses and models. One of the most recent commercial ventures of MSLO is the purchase of a wedding gift registry service and retailer.

In another arena—planning and celebrating weddings—MSLO took a step in a new direction. In March 2001 the corporation purchased Wedding List Holdings, Inc., a wedding gift registry service and retailer that operates an Internet website, *theweddinglist.com.* The registry service also has retail showrooms in New York, Boston, and London that allow guests and well-wishers of brides and grooms to purchase wedding gifts selected by the couple, without ever leaving their computer chairs. By combining MSLO products with an electronic gift registry, MSLO thus moved to make its products easily available to couples just starting to build a home.

Further expanding the merchandising end of its business, MSLO announced that it would expand its Martha Stewart Everyday Housewares product line with the spring 2001 launch of the Keeping (Organizing) category and the fall launch of the Decorating category, which would offer lamps, picture frames, and storage items. On television, MSLO continued its international expansion while developing new programs. And on the Internet, the company plans to redesign the look of its website and increase the number of products offered online.

Where to next?

When *Time* magazine chose Stewart as one of the 25 most influential people in America, Stewart gave a glimpse of her long-term plan. "It is our intention to own areas in communication. I don't mean to sound egomaniacal, but Perry Como [a popular singer and television personality during the 1950s] used to own Christmas on TV. By 'own' I mean monopolize and influence."

Evidently Stewart intends to continue spreading the Martha Stewart Living Omnimedia label and style across all forms of mass communication—radio, TV, the Internet, newspapers, and magazines. From making her own school dresses to becoming one of the wealthiest women in America, she has make good on the confidence expressed in the quote she chose for herself her high school yearbook:

"I do what I please and I do it with ease."

1941   Born Martha Kostyra in Jersey City, New Jersey, on August 3

1959   Graduates from high school and enrolls at Barnard College in New York

1961   Marries law student Andrew Stewart, son of a stockbroker

1964   Graduates from Barnard College

1965   Gives birth to daughter, Alexis

1967   Begins career as a stockbroker on Wall Street

1972   Moves with husband and daughter to Westport, Connecticut

1973   Leaves Wall Street during downturn in the economy

1976   Starts Market Basket, a catering business, at home

1982   Publishes *Entertaining*, her first of many successful cookbooks

1987   Develops a line of Martha Stewart products and becomes a "life-style consultant" for Kmart retail stores

1988   Divorces her husband

1991   Launches *Martha Stewart Living* magazine

1993   Launches half-hour TV show, *Martha Stewart Living*, for CBS

1995   Airs *Home for the Holidays*, TV special featuring First Lady Hillary Rodham Clinton

1996   Named one of "America's 25 Most Influential People" by *Time* magazine

1997   Is described negatively in unauthorized biography, *Martha Stewart— Just Desserts*, by Jerry Oppenhimer; buys out Time Inc.'s stake in *Martha Stewart Living*, taking complete control of the magazine; launches Martha Stewart Living Omnimedia, a conglomerate of her publishing, radio, television, and internet ventures

1998   Named one of the "50 Most Powerful Women" by *Fortune* magazine; receives James Beard Foundation Award for the Best National Cooking program; receives Edison Achievement Award from the American Marketing Association

1999   Named one of the "50 Most Powerful Women" for a second time by *Fortune* magazine; offers shares of Martha Stewart Living Omnimedia on the New York Stock Exchange for the first time

CHRONOLOGY

2000   Purchases 153-acre estate in Westchester County, New York, and
moves from home of nearly 30 years in Westport, Connecticut

2001   Receives sixth Daytime Emmy Award for her television program

Leadership Awards

1996   *Adweek* "Publishing Executive of the Year"
        Adweek Matrix Award (magazine category)
        Listed in *Times*'s "America's 25 Most Influential People"
        Listed among "New York's 100 Most Influential Women in
            Business" in *Crain's New York Business*

1998   Listed in *Fortune*'s "50 Most Powerful Women"
        Edison Achievement Award from the American Marketing
            Association
        HFN CEO Summit Award
        Inducted in National Sales & Marketing Hall of Fame

1999   Listed in *Fortune*'s "50 Most Powerful Women"
        HFN Top Lifestyle/Designer

2000   Listed in *Vanity Fair*'s Top 50 Leaders of the Information Age
        Named 274 on the annual "*Forbes* 400" list American
            Marketing Association
        Edison Achievement Award

Martha Stewart Living—Magazine Awards

1995   Listed number one on *Adweek*'s "Ten Hottest Magazines
            of 1995"

1996   Listed number two on *Adweek*'s "Ten Hottest Magazines
            of 1996"
        Advertising Age's "Magazine of the Year"

1997   Listed number two on *Adweek*'s "Ten Hottest Magazines
            of 1997"
        Listed number one on Capell's Circulation Report
            "Top 10" List

1998   Listed number two on Capell's Circulation Report
            "Top 10" list

ACCOMPLISHMENTS

Martha Stewart Living—Television Awards
Daytime Emmy Awards

1994–95   Outstanding Service Show Host
Outstanding Service Show

1996–97   Outstanding Service Show Host

1997–98   Outstanding Directing in a Service Show

1998–99   Outstanding Service Show

2000–01   Outstanding Service Show

Other Awards

1998   James Beard Foundation Award for the Best National
Cooking Segment

Books and Periodicals

Collins, Gail. "Martha, Martha." *McCall's*, October 1996.

"Martha Stewart: Empress of How-to." *Time*, June 17, 1996.

Meachum, Virginia. *Martha Stewart: Successful Businesswoman*. Berkeley Heights, N.J.: Enslow, 1998.

Perman, Stacy. "Attention K Martha Shoppers." *Time*, October 6, 1997.

Sirimarco, Elizabeth. *The Story of Martha Stewart Living*. Mankato, Minn.: Smart Apple Media, 2000.

Winfrey, Oprah. "Oprah Talks to Martha Stewart." *O, The Oprah Magazine*, September 2000.

Wooten, Sara M. *Martha Stewart*. Woodbridge, Conn.: Blackbirch Press, 1998.

Websites

American Academy of Achievement—Martha Stewart Profile
http://www.achievement.org/autodoc/page/ste0pro-1

marthastewart.com
http://www.marthastewart.com

Salon.com—"She's Martha and You're Not."
http://www.salon.com/bc/1999/02/cov_16bc3.html

INDEX

Abrams, Harry N. (publisher),
    Andy Stewart with, 46-47
American Express commer-
    cials, 81
askMartha (newspaper
    column), 17, 70, 71
askMartha (radio), 17, 70, 75

Barnard College, 29, 31-33,
    36, 37, 38
Beard, James, 50
Beard, James, Foundation
    Award, for *Martha Stewart
    Living* (television), 84
Becker, Marion Rombauer,
    50
Beers, Charlotte, 69, 76, 90
Bracken, Peg, 50
Breakfast in Bed (CD), 61
Brenner, Douglas, 98
Britannica.com, 89

Cablevision Systems Corp.,
    70
Cantitoe Corners
    (Westchester estate), 92-93
CBS, 70, 74
    *See also Martha Stewart
    Living* (television)
CBS This Morning
    (television), 74
Child, Julia, 50, 52, 67
Claibourne, Craig, 50
Clinton, Hillary Rodham, 72
Collier, Norma, 47-48
Connor, Tom, 80-81
Cooper-Hewitt Museum, 48
Country Living
    (magazine), 48
Crown Publishing Group,
    48-49, 50

Dennehy, Brian, 40
Didion, Joan, 92
Dinner for Two (CD), 61
Dolan, Charles F., 70
Drucker, Stephen, 15, 98
Dutch Boy paint, 59

Early Show, The
    (television), 74
Ekus, Lisa, 81
Emmy Awards, for *Martha
    Stewart Living*, 84
Emmy Awards, for
    Martha Stewart Living
    (television), 68
Entertaining (cookbook),
    48-52, 55

Family Circle (magazine), 48
Food Network, and
    Martha Stewart Living
    (television), 83

Gardening (magazine), 96
Glamour contest, 34
Goldstein, Lynda, 92
Great American Wreaths
    (book), 72

Hall, Floyd, 13, 14
Harper, Valerie, 38
Hawes, Elizabeth, 51, 52
House Beautiful
    (magazine), 48
Howard, Josefina, 68

Kmart
    and *Gardening*
        (magazine), 96
    Martha as life-style
        consultant for, 14, 87-89
    Martha's World in, 13-16,
        71, 74-75, 85, 100
Kostyra, Eddie (father),
    19-20, 21, 22, 24, 26,
    27-28, 32, 34, 35-36,
    51, 64
Kostyra, Eric (brother), 20
Kostyra, Kathy (sister), 25
Kostyra, Laura (sister), 25
Kostyra, Martha (mother),
    20-21, 22, 64, 76
Kwon, Beth, 83

Letterman, David, 81

McLaughlin, Patricia, 61,
    64, 90-91
Marie Claire (magazine), 34
Market Basket, 46, 47
Martha by Mail direct-mail
    catalog, 17, 71, 85
Martha Stewart Baby
    (magazine), 95, 96
marthastewart.com, 17, 70,
    71, 75-76, 85, 101
*Martha Stewart Cookbook,
    The*, 57
Martha Stewart Everyday
    Housewares, in Kmart,
    13-16, 71, 74-75, 85, 100
Martha Stewart Inc., 59
*Martha Stewart—Just Desserts:
    The Unauthorized Biography*
    (Oppenheimer), 76-77,
    79-80, 81
Martha Stewart Kids
    (magazine), 95
Martha Stewart Living
    (magazine), 15-16, 17,
    61-65, 70, 84
    and awards, 17
    Brenner replacing Drucker
        as editor of, 98
    and CDs, 98-99
    and competition, 96
    contents of, 63-64
    increased frequency of, 96
    launch of, 61-62
    and "Remembering," 21,
        27, 64, 87
    success of, 62-63, 64,
        71, 96
Martha Stewart Living
    (television), 67-68, 70,
    74, 84
    and awards, 17, 68, 84
    as daily program, 75
    extended format of, 83-84
    and Food Network, 83
    launch of, 67-68
    reruns of, 71
    studios for, 83-84
    and *Today* show, 67

Martha Stewart Living Enterprises, 72, 74
Martha Stewart Living Omnimedia (MSLO), 68-71, 72, 84-85
and buyout of Time Warner's stake in, 72, 74, 82
formation of, 68-71
organization of, 71
and Patrick, 69-71, 72, 74, 76, 82, 84, 96-97
as publicly traded stock on New York Stock Exchange, 81-83
and slowdown in magazine revenues, 96-98
success of, 84-85, 95
Martha Stewart's Christmas (book), 57, 61
Martha Stewart's Gardening Month by Month (book), 57
Martha Stewart's Healthy Quick Cook (cookbook), 57
Martha Stewart's Hors d'Oeuvres (cookbook), 55-56
Martha Stewart's Hors d'Oeuvres Handbook (cookbook), 57
Martha Stewart's Menus for Entertaining (cookbook), 57
Martha Stewart's New Old House (book), 57
Martha Stewart's Pies and Tarts (cookbook), 56-57
Martha Stewart's Quick Cook (cookbook), 55
Martha Stewart's Quick Cook Menus (cookbook), 57
Martha Stewart's Secrets of Entertaining (video), 59
Martha Stewart Weddings (magazine), 63, 96
Martha's World, in Kmart, 13-16, 71, 74-75, 85, 100

Mirken, Alan, 48-49
Mitchell, Miss, 24
Moses, Kate, 33, 64
MTV Music Awards, 81
Murdoch, Rupert, 62

Newhouse, S. I., 61-62
Newman, Paul and Joanne, 48
New Republic (magazine), 80
Newsweek (magazine), 52, 80
New York Times, 48
New York Times Magazine, 61, 64, 80, 90-91
Nutley High School, 26, 27, 28
Nutley Public Library, 24-25

Oppenheimer, Jerry, 76-77, 79-80, 81

Patrick, Sharon, 72, 74, 76, 84
and Martha Stewart Living Omnimedia, 69-71, 72, 74, 76, 82, 84, 96-97
and Stewart's perfectionism, 89
People (magazine), 48
Perman, Stacy, 74-75, 85
Potter, Clarkson N., 50, 51

Rainbow Programming Holdings Inc., 70
Reading Martha Stewart: It's a Good Thing (Smith and Goldstein), 92
Rhino Entertainment Company, 98
Rhymes, Busta, 81
Riman, Steve, 74
Ripp, Joseph, 74
Rombauer, Irma S., 50

Salon.com, 33, 39, 64, 91
Sherwin-Williams, 15, 71
Smith, Jaclyn, 58-59

Smith, Virginia, 92
Stewart, Alexis (daughter), 38, 40, 46, 88
Stewart, Andy (ex-husband), 33-34
as attorney, 38, 44, 45
and catering business, 48
and daughter, 88
and divorce, 60
and education, 33, 36-37
and *Entertaining* (cookbook), 51, 52
and family, 33-34, 38
with Harry N. Abrams (publisher), 46-47
and marriage, 35-36
Stewart, Diane (ex-sister-in-law), 33
Stewart, Martha
beliefs of, 92, 101
birth of, 19
and boyfriends, 28, 33-34
and catering business, 40, 46, 47-49, 89
and CD's and cassettes, 61, 98-99
and childhood, 19-26, 27, 64
and cooking classes, 46
critics of, 76-77, 79-81, 89-93
and daughter, 38, 40, 46, 88
and divorce, 60
and early culinary education, 37
and early jobs, 26-27, 28, 33, 34-35, 37
and early married life, 36-38
and East Hampton home, 14-15, 76, 84
education of, 22-24, 26, 27, 28-29, 31-33, 36, 37, 38
and entertaining, 36, 38
family of, 19-22, 23, 24, 25-26, 28, 34, 35-36, 64, 76

and first apartment, 36

and first Thanksgiving dinner, 36

and freelance writers, 50-51, 52

and future, 101

and gardening, 27, 39, 44

and "good thing," 67-68

and image, 48

and interior decorating, 36, 38-39, 40-41, 43-46, 44, 56

and leadership awards, 72, 101

and legal entanglements, 44, 52

as magazine food editor, 48

as maid, 34

marriage of, 35-36, 48, 60. *See also* Stewart, Andy

and Middlefield, Massachusetts schoolhouse, 38-39, 40, 44

as model, 26-27, 33, 34-35, 37, 38, 50

monetary worth of, 17, 83

and pets, 46

and reading, 24-25

and role models, 22-24

and second apartment, 38

and seminars on entertaining and decorating, 57

and sewing own clothes, 26, 29

as stockbroker, 39-40, 43, 45

and temper, 16, 80

and videos, 59

and wedding gift registry, 100

and Westchester County estate, 92-93

and Westport, Connecticut home. *See* Turkey Hill

Stuart, Katherine, 90

Thanksgiving Day special (TV), 57

Time (magazine), 74-75, 90

and Martha as one of "America's 25 Most Influential People," 72, 101

Time Warner, 71

and *Martha Stewart Living* (magazine), 62

and Martha Stewart Living Enterprises/ Omnimedia, 72, 74, 84

Today show, and *Martha Stewart Living* (television), 67

Tropp, Barbara, 52

Turkey Hill (Westport, Connecticut), 40-41, 72

and catering business, 40

and children's cooking classes, 46

and *Entertaining* (cookbook), 51

and Market Basket, 46

and *Martha Stewart's Christmas,* 61

move from, 85, 87-93

renovation of, 43-46, 47

and seminars on entertaining and decorating, 57

Uncatered Affair, An, 47-49, 89

Wakefield, Dan, 32

Wedding List Holdings, Inc., 100

Wedding Planner, The (book), 57, 61

Weddings (book), 59-60, 61

Westwood One Entertainment, 75

Weyer, Irene, 22-24

Williams, Mary Elizabeth, 39-40, 68, 91

Winfrey, Oprah, 16, 22, 31-32

Wolff, Anita, 89

Yantacaw Elementary School, 22-24

page

2: Everett Collection	37: New Millennium Images	82: Adam Nadel/AP/ Wide World Photos
12: Everett Collection	42: New Millennium Images	85: AFP/Corbis
16: Dave Allocca/ DMI/NMI	45: Everett Collection	86: New Millennium Images
18: ClassMates.Com Yearbook Archives	49: Ron Frehm/AP/ Wide World Photos	91: Barry Sweet/AP/ Wide World Photos
21: Michelle Fung/NMI	53: Everett Collection	93: David Allen/Corbis
23: Michelle Fung/NMI	54: New Millennium Images	94: Richard Drew/AP/ Wide World Photos
27: ClassMates.Com Yearbook Archives	58: Everett Collection	97: New Millennium Images
28: Michelle Fung/NMI	63: New Millennium Images	99: New Millennium Images
30: New Millennium Images	66: Davis Factor/Corbis	100: New Millennium Images
35: Sean Roberts/ Everett Collection	73: Photofest	102: Everett Collection
	75: New Millennium Images	
	78: New Millennium Images	

Cover Photo: New Millenium Images

Charles J. Shields was formerly the chairman of the guidance department at Homewood-Flossmoor High School in Flossmoor, Illinois. He currently writes full time from his home in Homewood, Illinois, where he lives with his wife, Guadalupe, an elementary school principal.

Matina S. Horner was president of Radcliffe College and associate professor of psychology and social relations at Harvard University. She is best known for her studies of women's motivation, achievement, and personality development. Dr. Horner has served on several national boards and advisory councils, including those of the National Science Foundation, Time Inc., and the Women's Research and Education Institute. She earned her B.A. from Bryn Mawr College and her Ph.D. from the University of Michigan, and holds honorary degrees from many colleges and universities, including Mount Holyoke, Smith, Tufts, and the University of Pennsylvania.